# Perspectives on

# Henderson Hospital

Edited by:

FIONA WARREN & BRIDGET DOLAN
Henderson Hospital
Sutton, Surrey.

Henderson Hospital (2001)

This edition is published in 2001 by:-

**HENDERSON HOSPITAL**
**2, Homeland Drive, Sutton, Surrey.**
**SM2 5LT**

*Henderson Hospital is part of South West London & St. George's Mental Health NHS Trust*

*ISBN     0 9526615*

# Contents

## *HENDERSON HOSPITAL OUTREACH SERVICE TEAM*

## *ANNOTATED BIBLIOGRAPHY*

# Introduction to the second edition

Fiona Warren & Bridget Dolan

The first *Perspectives on Henderson Hospital* was produced by Bridget Dolan in 1996 as an introduction to the clinical and research work of Henderson Hospital's therapeutic community. It proved to be very useful and popular both as a general introductory text and as a training tool. This second edition is divided into four sections covering the history, treatment model, treatment outcome and the Henderson Hospital Outreach Service Team (H.O.S.T) and is supplemented by an annotated bibliography of papers published between 1980 and 2000[1].

In the past four years since the publication of the first *Perspectives on Henderson Hospital*, Henderson has continued to produce research and clinical papers on personality disorders and associated issues, and the therapeutic community approach to treatment for this group. The hospital has also continued to contribute to training by providing study days, welcoming visitors on a weekly basis and by organising conferences on self-harm. These conferences sold out and there are continual requests for day visits to, and training by, Henderson Hospital which are testaments to the ongoing need for training and services for this client group. The 'Reed Committee' (a joint Home Office and Department of Health Review of Services for Mentally Disordered Offenders) highlighted the dearth of services nationally for people with severe personality disorders (Reed, 1992; Dolan and Coid, 1993) and its report recommended that *"more specialist units comparable to Henderson Hospital should be developed"* (Reed, 1994, p.43). In 1998, these recommendations were progressed when the National Specialist Commissioning Advisory Group to the government agreed specialist designation and central purchasing for the therapeutic community and its associated Henderson Outreach Service Team (HOST).  This agreement was also for the two-fold replication of this treatment approach.    Since then, Henderson Hospital has been collaborating with South Birmingham Mental Health NHS Trust and Mental Health Services of Salford NHS Trust to replicate this treatment setting in the Midlands and North West.    The new therapeutic communities, Main House and Webb House, and their associated outreach services open in late summer 2000.

The hospital predates the National Health Service, having started life in 1947 as the rehabilitation unit for veterans of WWII. The inception and early development of the community is recorded in detail by Maxwell Jones and Robert Rapoport (Jones, 1953; 1962; Rapoport, 1960). The papers in the present volume have been selected from those published since 1980 to reflect the more recent clinical and research practice at Henderson Hospital.

An historical account of the development of Henderson by Dr. Stuart Whiteley who was Medical Director of the unit between 1966 and 1989 opens this book. Whiteley (1980) charts the evolution of the Therapeutic Community through the 1940-1950's as Maxwell Jones' treatment approach rejected the more traditional, authoritarian, hierarchical style for a more collaborative staff-patient relationship which required internal re-organisation of the traditional hospital structures.  He describes the phases of development under different leadership and the contributions Henderson made to world knowledge of the therapeutic community model and the treatment of, what was then termed, 'psychopathic disorder'.  However, Whiteley also notes how the survival of the unit has continued to be at issue ever since its early establishment despite the successful outcome shown in the research studies conducted by himself and others.

The second section considers aspects of the treatment model as it is in practice today in two papers by Dr. Kingsley Norton, who succeeded Dr Whiteley in 1989, following his retirement.  Norton (1992) describes the current residents in the unit; the difficulty and importance of engaging these personality disordered clients in therapy; and how specific aspects of the model are arranged to facilitate a containing therapeutic environment. In the second paper, Norton (1992) considers how the structure and culture of the unit effect therapeutic change, relating the ideas and principles of Dr Tom Main, another progenitor of the therapeutic community model, to the present day Henderson Hospital.

As a "culture of enquiry", the therapeutic community, it is argued by Dolan *et al.* (1991), should be a model of treatment which is theoretically and practically equipped to address the institutionalised racism in British psychiatry. However, despite this theoretical ability and the publication of this paper, there continue to be relatively few referrals from ethnic minority groups for this treatment. Although not underrepresented in the staff team, ethnic minority groups continue to be underrepresented in the resident group, and there is anecdotal support for the idea that people from these groups are less likely to stay in treatment. Developments in recent years to explore these issues include an Ethnicity Task Group which has revised aspects of recruitment; employed an external consultant to provide race awareness training; invited speakers on this topic to academic meetings in the hospital and is developing links with groups for ethnic minorities in order to improve this situation[2].

The therapeutic community is also, theoretically, well-placed to manage impulsive, self-damaging and other acting out behaviours. The next paper in this volume discusses the way in which interactions between personality disordered individuals and institutions may perpetuate 'acting out' behaviour, if their complementary responses are not explored and understood (Norton and Dolan, 1995). Unpublished results of a more recent outcome study support the effectiveness of the TC in this respect, showing greater post-treatment reduction in self-damaging behaviours in a sample of referrals who attended the therapeutic community than those who were not admitted to the treatment (Warren *et al,* 1997).

The third section of the Volume comprises four recent studies of treatment outcome. Copas *et al.* (1984) demonstrate the long-term efficacy of admission to Henderson in terms of a notably lower rate of hospital admission and re-conviction five years subsequent to treatment. Residents admitted are compared with 51 people not admitted for treatment and a clear positive effect of admission and of length of stay is evident. This assessment of the more objective variables such as reduction in service usage is complemented by the study of Dolan *et al*. (1992) which shows a significant reduction in psychological distress following treatment in a shorter-term follow-up study. Another outcome study, begun in 1991 attempted to improve on the limitations of previous studies. The primary outcome measure for this study was core borderline personality disorder symptomatology. Very few treatment outcome studies of personality disorder have actually used personality disorder symptoms as an outcome measure. Dolan *et al* (1997) demonstrates a highly significant treatment effect on these symptoms at one year follow-up.

Changes in the management and funding arrangements of the British National Health Service, which were implemented in April 1991, had a significant, detrimental impact upon the provision of specialist treatment in units such as Henderson Hospital. "Value for money" seemed to become a guiding principle of the NHS, with psychotherapy, and inpatient psychotherapy in particular, often considered expensive luxuries. The final paper in this section by Dolan *et al.* (1996) focuses upon the costs of treatment in Henderson Hospital. This paper provides follow-up data on the group from which Menzies *et al.* (1993) extrapolated and shows that the cost of treatment can be expected to be recouped in 2 years post treatment. It is notable that the cost-offset predicted in Menzies study was shown by the actual offset to be a conservative estimate.

The final section comprises a paper describing the first year of operation of Henderson Hospital's innovative Outreach Service which was developed in 1995 in response to audit findings (Morant et al, 1999). Operating on a small staff complement of 2.4 wte clinicians, the service aimed to provide preparation for and follow-up after, the inpatient service, as well as alternative outpatient treatment and management advice to clinical teams. The paper describes the patient characteristics and the first year's clinical activity.

These papers are selected to provide a general introduction for the reader to aspects of the history, theory, practice, research and outcome of treatment in the unit. It is hoped that the annotated bibliography of publications from Henderson Hospital between 1980 and 2000 will guide readers to further papers which will be of relevance to their particular interests.

## REFERENCES

DOLAN, B. & COID, J. (1993) *Psychopathic and Anti-social Personality Disorders: Treatment and Research Issues.* Gaskell, London

DOLAN, B. WARREN, F. & NORTON, K. (1997) Change in borderline symptoms one year after therapeutic community treatment for severe personality disorder. *British Journal of Psychiatry* 171, 274-279

JONES, M. (1962) *Social Psychiatry in the Community, in Hospitals and in Prisons.* Charles C. Thomas, Springfield Illinois.

JONES, M. (1953) *The Therapeutic Community: A New Treatment Method in Psychiatry.* Basic Books, New York

MENZIES, D., DOLAN, B. & NORTON, K. (1993) Funding treatment for personality disorders: Are short term savings worth long term costs? *Psychiatric Bulletin,* Vol. 17, 517-519.

MORANT, N., DOLAN, B., FAINMAN, D. & HILTON, M.(1999) An Innovative Outreach Service for People With Severe Personality Disorders : Patient Characteristics and Clinical Activities. *Journal of Forensic Psychiatry:* Vol. 10: No 1: pp. 84-97.

RAPOPORT, R. (1960) *Community as Doctor.* London, Tavistock

REED, J. (1992) *Review of Services for Mentally Disordered Offenders and Others with Similar Needs.* London, HMSO.

REED, J. (1994) *Report of the joint Department of Health and Home Office Working Group on Psychopathic Disorder.* London, HMSO.

WARREN, F. EVANS, C, DOLAN, B. & NORTON, K. (1997) *Impulsivity in personality disorders:* One year outcome. Presentation at 5th International Conference on Personality Disorders (Vancouver).

[1] Some key papers published pre-1980 are also included in the bibliography.

[2] For further information about the ethnicity group or to discuss referrals for whom this may be an issue, please contact the hospital.

# The Henderson Hospital
## A Community Study

J. Stuart Whiteley

*International Journal of Therapeutic Communities*
*1980, Vol. 1(1): pp 38-58*

The historical development of the therapeutic community at Henderson Hospital is described with particular reference to the contribution the hospital has made to world psychiatry in both the area of the therapeutic community and the treatment of psychopaths. The three decades which the hospital has spanned are viewed in terms of the over-riding theme of each decade and also as a reflection of the pertaining leadership. Maxwell Jones was the first leader and his concept of the therapeutic community stems from his work at Henderson which continues to be a source of influence in current psychiatric practice.

## INTRODUCTION

The Henderson Hospital was so named in 1959 when it became established as an autonomous unit. The naming was in honour of Professor D.K. Henderson who had been Maxwell Jones' mentor in the Department of Psychiatry at the University of Edinburgh and who was the author of *Psychopathic States* (Henderson, 1939).

From 1947 to 1959 the unit had been geographically and administratively a wing of the larger Belmont Hospital, a Neurosis Centre. In these early days there was interest in the unit, but there developed a certain amount of friction and conflict between the main hospital and its more orthodox stance and the innovative unit of Maxwell Jones. From 1959 onwards, when the ideological separation was clearer (and the patients in the unit became more diagnostically differentiated as psychopaths or character disorders) the conflict was less overt. But there continued to be undercurrents of hostility, suspicion and rivalry locally even though in the wider world the hospital with its methods had gained acceptance and indeed acclaim.

In 1974 the old Belmont Hospital was vacated and its patients were moved to a new unit some distance away. But, still the uneasy working relationship has continued on the home front so that Henderson always appears the wayward daughter to its critical elder sister across the way, now an acute psychiatry unit.

In 1977 the Henderson moved out of the remains of the old building and into a relatively modern accommodation to which was added a recreational complex (gym, squash court and billiard room). Half of this was funded by a number of Charitable Trusts which expressed a belief in the work of the unit. Residents of Henderson today enjoy single room accommodation with good furnishings, a large working and leisure garden, workshops, living and recreational space. The atmosphere is much more that of a students' hostel or a residential training course than a hospital. Contrary to the expectation of critics, the building has been respected and valued by the residents, who have added to its amenities by various fund-raising exercises.

It is ironic that, as the first issue of the *International Journal of Therapeutic Communities* goes to press and Henderson is honoured by being invited to be the first therapeutic community to assess its work and influence in world psychiatry, that it is once more under threat of closure.

Henderson has always attracted curious and critical attention and from a public relations point a view felt the need to put itself forward for scrutiny. Consequently, the Visitors' Day started by Maxwell Jones in the 50's continues to draw some 250 people a year. Longer term visitors come for two week periods from various social work, psychology, nursing or probation training schemes. But doctors number few in visitor lists and the old professional interest (but polite non-committal) prevails. It is in the hostel or social work field rather than the hospital that the therapeutic community method seems to find more support.

A number of newspaper and magazine articles have appeared written by journalists and these have been fulsome or critical but seldom grasping the complexities of the Henderson therapeutic community.

A documentary film was made by an American based company about the first Belmont community reflecting the US interest. And more recently four TV films have been made. But these too have had a mixed reception from the general public where ideas remain firmly fixed for or against what is seen still as an unorthodox treatment approach despite the widespread assimilation of some basic therapeutic community ideas into contemporary society.

The story of Henderson over the last 30 years can conveniently be divided into three decades encompassing in turn: 1947-57, The Ideas; 1957-67, The Theory; 1967-onward, The Practice.

## THE IDEAS: 1947-57

The first decade was concerned with ideas, of which there was no shortage. Professor Sir Aubrey Lewis, the holder of what was then the only Chair in Psychiatry in England, comments in his introduction to *Social Psychiatry* (Jones et al., 1952) on the "unremitting energy, sustained purpose and enthusiasm which he (Jones) has put into this difficult enterprise". It is interesting to note that the sub-title of this book "A study of therapeutic communities" was inserted at the request of the American publishers because at that time the USA, in the grip of anti-Communist McCarthyism, was suspect of anything which inferred a Socialist outlook.

The roots of Henderson extend back into the three transitional communities that the above volume described. The first of these was the Effort Syndrome Unit at Mill Hill Military Hospital in London. It was established with the backing of Lewis in 1941 and Maxwell Jones was seconded from the Maudsley as co-director with a cardiologist, Paul Wood. The experience here showed Jones the strength of peer-group support in large group situations, how clear communications were able to disperse anxiety and doubts which led to symptoms and the value of fellow patients in passing on the culture and the message to new admissions. Small group discussions were instituted usually with a selected topic and led by a doctor and they were both educational (in regard to the origin of symptoms) and philosophical in directing the patients to consider problems in the wider social milieu of their life and times. In 1945 a similar regime was adopted by Jones in a unit for emotionally disturbed P.O.W.s returned from the Far East. Here the value of patients' committee to run the day to day affairs of the Unit was discovered and this itself originated from the management committees set up by the soldiers in the former Prison Camps. The total push methods directed at getting these "displaced" and disadvantaged men back into work or social activities pointed the way to how similar methods may be used with the industrial misfit who drifted aimlessly from job to job and in 1947 the Ministry of Labour set up the Industrial Rehabilitation Unit at Belmont on an experimental basis. Once more Lewis and the Maudsley Hospital backed Maxwell Jones in this project which was carefully researched and a succession of trainee psychiatrists returning from army service began to pass through the unit and gain experience of the therapeutic community. The patients were neurotics, often chronically disabled and unable to maintain a job, those with character disorders or borderline psychotic illnesses and the idea behind the experiment was that just as in war-time a useful place had been found for many social misfits and neurotic casualties so in peace-time could they be helped to find resources within themselves to lead more fulfilling lives.

As one reads *Social Psychiatry* today it often appears naïve and simplistic but one cannot but be astounded at how much of lasting psychological and sociological import was stumbled upon in these early days, the value realised and similar situations promoted. At that time group psychotherapy was in its infancy. It is clear from the paucity of references in the early papers and the book that few ideas were being imported from elsewhere. Even though Main had developed his "therapeutic institution" ideology at Northfield Military Hospital, in Birmingham, there was very little, if any, cross fertilisation to Mill Hill and similarly with Foulkes' early experiments in group therapy also at Northfield. Yet, in 1942, Maxwell Jones published an article on *Group Psychotherapy* and in 1949 on *Acting as an Aid in the Treatment of Neurosis*. This latter aspect developed without any knowledge of Moreno or his work but emanated from educational sketches acted by the nurses to illustrate a point. Once more it came to be realised that the psychodrama was of much more value if the patients acted out real life situations that had emotional content for themselves.

Moreno later paid many visits to Belmont and several actors attended the psychodrama sessions. The Unity Theatre in London actually incorporated one presentation into their repertory programme.

In the Industrial Rehabilitation Unit Dr. Baker is described introducing a role-playing style of working into his groups whilst Dr. Merry is shown in a more interpretative, although nonetheless directive style. The utilisation of brief acting through situations in the small group discussions when words failed was described in a way that we might now label as Rogerian or Gestalt.

Baker later became Director of the Hospital Advisory Service and Merry the Director of an Alcoholic Unit utilising therapeutic community methods and similarly did many of the trainee doctors at Belmont make a mark in post war psychiatry. Lambo, in 1953, became Deputy Director of the World Health Organisation. At Belmont he had likened the culture to that of a Nigerian village with its strong peer group ties[1]. Pomryn (1950-1957) started the therapeutic community at Littlemore Hospital, Oxford which remains to this day one of the forerunners of the therapeutic community in the general psychiatric field. Eileen Skellern, Sister in Charge (from 1952 to 1957) became the Superintendent of Nursing at the Maudsley Hospital (Institute of Psychiatry) in 1959 and remained there until her retirement in 1979.

At this stage the unit for all its democratic strivings and shared responsibilities was still firmly held in the doctor and nursing meritocracy. Merry is 'applauded' by the group for some particularly clever interpretation for which they are duly grateful and the nurses are instructed in their caring and intermediary function between doctors and patients. It is they who must instil into their charges the values of the unit.

Nevertheless, in comparison with the very medical model then prevalent in other mental hospitals and the largely custodial role of the nurses therein the awareness of the social milieu at Belmont and how this could be turned to good effect was far ahead of its time. It was only in 1954 that Stanton and Schwartz published *The Mental Hospital* directing attention to the milieu and then followed the similar books by Caudill, Belknap, the Cummings, Goffman etc. Although drugs and ECT were originally used in

---

[1] See also: Azu-Okeke (1992) cited in the annotated bibliography

the unit, by 1950 it was found that they could be dispensed with and two nurses covered the unit at night depending on support from the patient group of 90 or so individuals.

In the early 1950's Maxwell Jones work was recognised outside of the UK and he was appointed a Consultant in Mental Health to the World Health Organisation with the task of preparing a report on Rehabilitation. He began to tour Europe, the USA, Africa and Australasia discovering the social psychiatry methods of Querido in Amsterdam, for instance, and other social psychiatry ventures such as Wilmer's which had developed in a US Navy Hospital during the war and which after his visit to Belmont in 1950 turned more to the therapeutic community model. The exchange of ideas and of visits was salutary on both sides. Whilst Jones' methods in the therapeutic community were taken up in many places, notably Scandinavia (e.g. the University Clinic at Ulleval in Oslo) he began to refer widely to these newly discovered social psychiatry experiences from overseas in this writings and lectures. He visited Herstedvester in Denmark, the Children's Village in Stockholm and the Rehabilitation Centre in Oslo and found he was acting as a catalyst to their developing ideas in social and community psychiatry. A visit to East Berlin had little impact but in Sweden he was called a Marxist!

A World Health Organisation report asked the question of Belmont and Maxwell Jones "how much was the method and how much the man?"

Jones was awarded the CBE in 1954 in connection with his work on Rehabilitation and his ten years of service on the National Advisory Council of the Ministry of Labour. Having produced the report on Rehabilitation for the World Health Organisation (WHO/Ment/30) and also served on the board of the Tavistock Institute of Human Relations for ten years where he became familiar with the work of Trist and others in industry and organisations he felt that the creative therapeutic work at Belmont was ahead of any other unit in this field throughout the world.

The Industrial Rehabilitation Unit with its emphasis on resettlement in work changed its name to the Social Rehabilitation Unit in 1954 when it began to be realised that the inability to settle in a job was due more to lack of social and interpersonal skills than to any lack of industrial or educational expertise. An example of this change of emphasis was the ex-patients social club which started at St. George's Hospital in Central London in 1949, possibly the first of its kind.

More and more patients now came to the Unit from the Courts or through Rehabilitation Officers and Social Work agencies to which they had finally drifted down and been labelled as social inadequates and the numbers with criminal records began to increase.

Towards the mid-fifties therefore the Unit was developing into two areas of specialisation (1) as the centre of the therapeutic community ideology and (2) as a treatment unit for psychopaths.

Back home Jones was under pressure to prove the method had substance and value. However, no social scientists in the UK were interested in exploring the milieu of the mental hospital, despite the considerable interest that was being shown in this topic in the USA. At this point in time Maxwell Jones met a young social anthropologist at a cocktail party in Boston. Robert Rapoport had just concluded a study of the Navajo Indians and was looking for a new project. Maxwell Jones secured a substantial grant from the Nuffield Foundation and in 1954 the work that was to dominate the next decade in the history of the Henderson began.

**THE THEORY : 1957-67**

Rapoport spent 1954 in the Belmont Social Rehabilitation Unit gathering his research team and planning the project. Originally it was intended to be the evaluative study of the treatment of psychopaths for which the critics of Maxwell Jones and his method were calling. However, such was the controversy over the diagnostic use of the term "psychopath" that the study changed direction and became instead an in-depth exploration of the workings of a therapeutic community. This continued until 1957 when the writing began.

There was one joint paper from Maxwell Jones and Robert Rapoport on *Administrative and Social Psychiatry* (1955) which is virtually a review of *The Mental Hospital* (Stanton and Schwartz, 1953) but, thereafter, researcher and clinician went in separate directions and one gathers that the atmosphere between the research and the clinical teams was, at times, fraught.

A flood of scientific papers emanated from the Rapoport team in a number of English and American journals, psychiatric and psychological, sociological, psychoanalytic and nursing.  These were the papers that laid bare the social interactions on the ward, examined leadership, the cycles of organisation and disorganisation, democratisation and authority, role theory in the hospital and in the family and in delinquent behaviour and permissiveness and the problems that may arise for staff and patients in consequence.

These were the key papers that both underpinned the therapeutic community as a treatment modality but, also, threatened to undermine it as the weaknesses of the system were pointed out.

The authors of these papers read like an Alma Mater role of honour - Robert and Rhona Rapoport, Seymour Parker, Terence Morris, Pauline Morris, Gillian Elles, Irvine Rosow, Joy Tuxford, et al.

The studies themselves were gathered together to form the basis of *Community as Doctor* first published in 1960 and in an interesting reflection on its first and later impact as a research report Manning and Rapoport (1976) made a number of observations in a follow-up paper.

The book had a mixed reception in 1960 and was not reviewed in many leading American and British anthropological or sociological journals. In those where it was reviewed the sociological aspect was often played down. Psychiatrists, however, seemed to review the work fairly well although assimilating both the positive and negative aspects of the therapeutic community that it had clarified.

However, reception of the study back a Belmont (re-named Henderson Hospital in 1959) was largely critical. Maxwell Jones, himself, had left to take up an appointment in the USA in 1959.  The Unit was once more under threat of closure with demands to justify its unorthodox method of working and some of the basic staff who had served through the traumas of being researched upon felt aggrieved and dishonoured by the text and in addition perhaps deserted by their leader.  The new director (Taylor) reviewed the book for the Journal of Mental Science (later British Journal of Psychiatry) and was somewhat dismissive.

Within the unit there were those who rejected the book and its findings and needed to cling on to the old slogan based ideologies (and these were often newly joined staff).  There were those who implicitly accepted some of the basic sociodynamic findings and began to build into the Henderson both a more realistic and less intuitively based style and a rather mechanistic network of interactions for subsequent commentary and exploration. Stallard (later Consultant Psychiatrist, Douglas Inch Clinic, Glasgow) was foremost in this latter and under his tutelage the more formalised but responsibility-sharing structure of patient committees emerged as did the jointly working group of staff and patients to select new patients for admission. This selection procedure has been copied widely by hostels and other therapeutic communities but is one of the most controversial aspects of the therapeutic community in so far as it raises alarm and misgivings in the breasts of the professionally conscious opponents of the method.

One of the Rapoport findings was that the therapeutic community method was not universally applicable as Maxwell Jones had believed. Some selection was necessary. Those with weak ego-structure could be further damaged by the intensive social and inter-personal pressures.

Rapoport also pointed out the conflict between the psychotherapeutic and treatment aims of the medical staff and the rehabilitatory aims of the lay workshop instructors.

Maxwell Jones (1968) later commented that "for me to discover the discrepancy between what I thought I was doing as a leader and what trained observers saw me doing was frequently a painful - but almost invariably a rich - learning experience".

Jones had been more concerned with psychopathic disorder in the late fifties and his efforts to propound a treatment regime resulted in a number of papers on the subject and a gradual shift in the patient population towards that diagnostic category and away from the chronically inadequate neurotic. He gave written and oral evidence to the Royal Commission looking at the Mental Health Act and advocated the setting-up of special units to treat psychopaths.

However, although psychopathic disorder was included in the revised Act in 1959 largely on Jones' advice and special treatment units were envisaged therein, none were built and the legislation has in fact proved relatively useless. This is because psychopathic disorder remains an ill-defined and controversial topic. The new legislation was opposed by many liberal-minded groups and so beset by safe-guards and provisos that it became meaningless.

Maxwell Jones had envisaged a range of treatment approaches (open and closed units in hospitals) and a closed prison unit such as East and Hubert (1939) had described in the mid-thirties.

His excursions into the penal field resulted in Professor Baan of the Department of Criminology at Utrecht setting up a Psychopathic Unit in Holland at the Van der Hoeven Clinic and sending staff to Belmont for initial training. The California Department of corrections was much influenced by his contact and Dennie Briggs after a period at Belmont set up a therapeutic community in a maximum security prison at Chino. Governor Earl Warren of California (later Chief Justice of the Supreme Court) sent over his secretary to study the Belmont methods.

The staff of the newly opened Grendon Underwood prison for psychopathic offenders also began to attend Henderson for training placements from about 1962 onwards. The population of the Henderson became a more delinquent one as the interests of the new Director (Taylor, a former prison doctor) and his deputy (Stallard) were in the field of delinquency and its treatment. Training groups were conducted by Henderson staff at Holloway Prison for Women and at a Borstal for young offenders. One of the female staff later became an Assistant Governor of Holloway Prison (Smith, 1966) whilst more than one nurse turned to the Probation Service (particularly in prison liaison work) for a future career.

In 1959 Maxwell Jones was awarded the Isaac Ray Award by the American Psychiatric Association (the first non-American to be so honoured) and became Commonwealth Visiting Professor in Psychiatry at the University of Stanford from 1959-60, as well as delivering a series of lectures at the University of Washington, later published in *Social Psychiatry in the Community, in Hospitals and in Prisons* (Jones, 1962). Thereafter he worked at Oregon State Hospital as Director of Education and was Research and Clinical Professor at he University of Oregon. He was now lecturing and writing extensively and visiting and influencing a number of hospitals, penal institutions and community projects in North America. He returned to Dingleton Hospital, Scotland in late 1962 where his own interests began to extend beyond the hospital based therapeutic community (Jones, 1968).

Meanwhile, back at the Henderson work continued in a lower key. When the unit became autonomous in 1959 it became necessary to provide nursing cover for the unit from its own staff.   Therefore, some of the untrained social therapist posts had to be lost to nursing posts.   Elizabeth Barnes (the new matron) contributed to nursing education through publications and by setting up a nurse training programme in therapeutic community methods. Gill Elles, who stayed on from the research team, developed work with families.  The Unit survived to the mid-sixties, not as much in the spotlight, and rather rigid in its functioning by the rule book, but in some ways more democratic and less leader dependent.

Visitors from overseas continued to come to Henderson for long and short visits.  In particular there was a steady supply of young social work students from Sweden, Denmark and Norway to fill the short-term social therapist posts, which Maxwell Jones had originally set up in 1948 following a visit from a Norwegian social worker, in an attempt to break away from the routinised nurse-patient interactions so indigenous to the hospital situation.  Whilst the Scandinavian social work schools pressed enthusiastically for the social therapist training places at Henderson, there were few if any applicants from the more academically structured and theoretically based UK colleges.   Once again Belmont pioneered the employment of "non-professionals" in the mental health and social services field.

In 1965 Taylor left to become the first Director of a newly built acute psychiatry hospital in Birmingham, the John Conolly, which became a successful therapeutic community although not without its crises of leadership and self-examination of its functions.  Stallard who had held the fort in various leadership gaps in the past left soon afterwards for a Consultant post at the Douglas Inch Clinic, Glasgow.

On the whole the therapeutic community idea began to fade in the mid-sixties in the UK although in the USA, Scandinavia and Holland it was picking up an impetus of its own and developing a variety of ways.  Once more the question of the continuation of the unit was raised by the Regional administration.

**THE PRACTICE: 1967-PRESENT**

In 1966 the present author took over as Medical Director of Henderson and a new matron was also appointed from the Cassel Hospital whence had come the two previous senior nursing officers.

The Regional Hospital Board were obviously ambivalent about the unit and its work which was still regarded as "unevaluated" but, after initiating the secondment of the author to this post on a temporary basis because of his known interest in group psychotherapy and in the treatment of delinquents, the Regional Hospital Board elected to give the new team some backing and allow possible developments to go ahead.

The Unit was now firmly regarded as a treatment centre for delinquents and the therapeutic community aspect was secondary. Thus, the proportion of those patients with a history of conviction in a 1965 survey was 66% compared with 37% in 1955.

*Studies in Delinquency*
The first lecturing and writing engagements for Whiteley were in the prison and probation areas and the first major publication was an attempt to evaluate the response of psychopaths to therapeutic community treatment (1970). This work was undertaken whilst the author held a Cropwood Fellowship at the Institute of Criminology in Cambridge.

Its findings were that approximately 40% of the patients treated at Henderson did not relapse within a two to three year period in terms of further hospitalisation or criminal conviction. Furthermore, it pointed the way to the differentiation of personality types within the broad category of psychopathic disorder and the differing responses of those different types to the treatment process. Other findings were as follows.

Prognostic factors indicative of a good outcome were evidence of a previous ability to achieve success in school, work or interpersonal relationships together with evidence of a capacity for emotional feeling and involvement in the living community affairs. The therapeutic community of the highly differentiated dynamic and stressful type as at Henderson was of benefit to the sociopath who was not grossly emotionally immature and has some potential for personality growth ("creative psychopath") in a stimulating and permissive environment. It was of less benefit and could be harmful to the more immature, persistently acting out sociopath ("inadequate psychopath") and it is doubtful if it can be of benefit to the totally egocentric, impulsive, thought disordered and primitive personality ("aggressive psychopath").

This theme of a continuum of different stages in personality development requiring different social networks in which to grow and adversely affected by inappropriate "living and learning" situation which threatened rather than encouraged growth was followed up in the book *Dealing with Deviants* (Whiteley et al., 1972). A co-author was Dennie Briggs, now returned to Henderson from his work in the California Department of Corrections. The book describes the intensive and sophisticated therapeutic community at Henderson, a community in a maximum security prison and, in between, a supportive aftercare hostel for recidivist prisoners.

There were direct links between the Belmont Unit of Maxwell Jones and Briggs' work in Chino Prison and a shared philosophy of treatment between Whiteley and Turner who founded the after-care hostel described. Not only had Whiteley worked briefly with Turner but more than one resident had passed through the two units at different epochs in their lives.

D.K. Henderson's description of the aggressive, inadequate and creative psychopaths were thus re-affirmed more clinically and the appropriate treatment settings were described.

The objective appraisal of the results of treatment and identification of the types likely to respond has continued through further long term studies. A Predictive Equation (Copas and Whiteley, 1976) was formulated and validated giving weighted values to the positive and negative prognostic factors and an interesting finding was that whereas uncomplicated criminal or psychiatric histories were basically of poor prognosis, when there was an admixture of the two this could be advantageous to the outcome of treatment, presumably indicating an "affective" or emotional component in the offending which then made the subject open to therapeutic community treatment.

O'Brien (1976) in a detailed psychological study identified four major types of patients at Henderson; the anxious intropunitive (neurotic), anxiety-free extropunitive (psychopathic), anxious extropunitive, and anxiety-free intropunitive.

A follow up study under way indicates that the Henderson therapeutic community approach is of particular benefit to the anxiety free-intropunitive group which again draws attention to the need for something between penal and a psychiatric management for a type of personality who somehow falls between the pure criminal and the pure psychiatric patient[2].

These studies emphasised the need for the positive selection of patients and over the years the population under treatment changed to a less recidivist group, still offenders, but earlier in their offending careers, with more positive personality attributes and hence more prospect of success. By 1979 the proportion of patients with a conviction was 43%.

The change took place very slowly but, to the chagrin of the probation officers who had always felt there was hope for their more disturbed or inadequate clients at Henderson.

*Progress in the therapeutic community*
In 1967 *Community as Doctor* was re-issued and this time had a better reception. The wider influence of the book and the study it described is referred to in the Manning and Rapoport review (1976). The overall climate had changed to a more socially conscious one and this was reflected in psychiatric practice. Whilst it is true that general psychiatry had retreated into the medical model with the advent of new pharmacological products there was also a strong undercurrent of the social psychiatry and group awareness which Maxwell Jones and his team had forerun in the early post war years. *Community as Doctor* was brought back into Henderson as a teaching guide by the new team and attention was turned again to the psychological and sociological dynamics of the therapeutic community.

There was a general move at Henderson towards a greater observation of the principles enunciated in Rapoport's postulates since we observed that some of the same issues and problems of the early study still remained. The new staff were less concerned with the old days and thereby more flexible and open to change. We moved from the rehabilitatory end of the spectrum toward the treatment goal and introduced a more consciously psychodynamic and sociodynamic perspective. In particular the old workshop instructors were put aside and nurses took over these posts

---

[2] See: Copas *et al.*, (1984) in this volume

bringing more psychological awareness if less technical skill to the jobs around the house. We let the Scandinavian influx fade and encouraged home universities and colleges to send their students for training placements and gradually became more role specific and conscious of the need for specialised training in group work in small, large and activity based groups.

In *Dealing with Deviants* attention was paid to the concept of the total community as one on-going therapeutic group with its sub-divisions serving different functions but the large group being the keystone of the therapeutic community. It was shown how Whitaker and Leiberman's Group Focal Conflict theory (1965) had particular application in such a group where interpersonal and social behaviour was more to the fore than intra-personal conflicts and emotional disturbance, in which a more psychoanalytic approach may be more appropriate.

Manor (1979) examined roles undertaken by the patients as part of the sociotherapeutic process and was able to point out which jobs undertaken by the patients in their progress through the network of community posts encouraged most change in a positive direction. Thus, the service jobs (catering assistant, etc.) produced little change and even deterioration in isolated or deviant behaviour. The authoritarian jobs, such as chairman, merely reinforced authoritarian attitudes, whilst the "creative" posts which had few of the trappings of power, more freedom to experiment and, perhaps, little expectation, promoted most personality growth and development. These jobs were ward representative, workshop leader, social work assistant, etc. Thus, a form of sociotherapy was being clarified which although different in approach and application was not wholly separated from the psychotherapeutic process as is described in Edelson's model (1970). Instead, a skilful blend of sociotherapy and psychotherapy was aimed at in the Henderson, particularly appropriate to the treatment of patients in a residential setting and the differences from the Edelson model are described by Whiteley in a chapter in *The Large Group* (Kreeger, 1975).

Re-examination of staff roles in the Henderson (Whiteley & Zlatic, 1972) had shown that whatever the professed allegiance to the therapeutic community ideology, when under pressure from the patient group or insecure in the staff group, the various staff members tended to fall back on their traditional professional roles, e.g. the nurse to surgery and ward office duties or the doctor to medical interventions which could not be questioned by the layman.

Manning, who visited Henderson briefly to add to a thesis on Social Psychiatry but stayed on for two years (to our delight), reopened some of the investigations carried out by Rapoport and his team. During his stay at Henderson and through the informal contact afterwards he has continued to bring a sociological viewpoint to the examination of therapeutic communities. Like Rapoport he is not uncritical, believing that the therapeutic community was an innovative phenomenon of a particular epoch when psychiatry needed such a boost and that institutionalisation and routinisation (which was a feature of the second decade) has robbed it of its impetus and continuing effectiveness, (Manning, 1976a).

Nevertheless, like Rapoport he has remained close to the heart of the therapeutic community and intrigued by it in his subsequent work. In one study (Manning, 1976b) he compared the staff and patient preferences for the treatment situations available in the Rapoport era with those in the present decade. He found that although the individual doctor-patient interview had gone (and thus lost its primary importance) it had been replaced by the doctor led small psychotherapy group in the order of preference, despite a generally professed increased allegiance to the large group and therapeutic community ideology. Thus, he affirms that there is a gap between values and practice in the therapeutic community which has actually widened over the years due to generation of group norms and other informal processes, the need for innovation and the pursuit of an ideal having been lost.

This values and practice gap is perhaps further highlighted in two more recent papers. Despite the early decade's strivings toward a peer group culture and the definite egalitarian drive of the second decade, in the present decade there has been a re-emergence of leadership roles both in the therapeutic community as a whole and in the various sub-groups. But it is emphasised that this is to be understood in terms of a transference phenomenon and also as a normal group dynamic and by being brought into awareness it can be used in the therapeutic process (Whiteley, 1978).

In a brief study utilising the Moos Ward Atmosphere Scale (Moos, 1974) soon after moving into new premises we also showed how increasing the clarity and order functions in the community, by giving clear instructions about what was expected of staff and patients in their various roles about the house we did not undermine the therapeutic community as some had foretold, but actually enhanced the relationship functions of the group, presumably by clarifying boundaries and expectations and freeing those concerned from pointless uncertainty and anxiety (Whiteley, 1979).

The workings of the therapeutic community were most importantly questioned in 1971 when a meeting was called at the Henderson to examine the then present state of the therapeutic community. There were 12 invited participants all of whom had written of, researched into or had great experience of the therapeutic community. The meeting was such a successful sharing of ideas that enthusiasm for the therapeutic community revived in the UK. Further meetings were called for and the Round Table, as it was named, began to visit other therapeutic communities for its deliberations. Such was the clamour for a place at the Table that we had no choice but to open the meetings to all staff employed or interested in therapeutic community ideas and in 1972 the Association of Therapeutic Communities (ATC) was formed.

Henderson has continued to be a somewhat idealised focal point in the Association. Initially, the secretary of the Association was located there and enquiries came in from UK and abroad about therapeutic community methods, training opportunities or simply the sharing of ideas and opinions. The interest in Henderson, nationally and internationally, revived along with the interest in therapeutic communities. Major contact with the Dutch VWPG ensued from visits to the ATC meetings and to Henderson by staff from Santpoort and other Netherlands therapeutic communities. This resulted in an annual conference at Windsor from 1978 onwards. Zeigenfuss, researching rather isolatedly in the USA, also made contact and gained encouragement which broadened his own enquiries. Correspondents from Yugoslavia, New Zealand, South Africa and other centres in North America made contact with the ATC through Henderson Hospital.

The ATC has undoubtedly influenced the resurgence of many therapeutic community wards and community based projects and through its own conception at the Henderson-inspired Round Table meetings it can be said that the Henderson promoted this further wave of therapeutic community application in the 70's.

Similarly, personal contact between David Wills (and the Planned Environment Therapy Trust) and Whiteley (and the ATC) not only through a shared philosophy but also through a shared (and successful) patient as boy and man resulted in a move for the ATC to work collaboratively with the Planned Environment Therapy Trust toward an annual conference and to propose a training scheme and qualification for social therapists. Henderson staff have been the key figures in this cross-boundary liaison between hospitals, schools and hostels.

*The Wider Practice*
Thus, taken together the various Henderson studies of the past decade identify a group of individuals neither distinctly criminal nor obviously mentally ill but presenting a problem of management for both penal and medical services. They are shown to respond well to the blend of sociotherapy and psychotherapy which has evolved in this originating therapeutic community by a move towards greater self-reliance and less anti-social behaviour and some of the crucial interventions and mechanisms have been clarified.

On the basis of this in 1976, the Henderson began an annual course in Group Work for hospital staff, Probation Officers and residential social workers, which took in a broad base of group analytic, therapeutic community, encounter and experiential groups and derived from both psychodynamic theory and group dynamic (i.e. the social dynamics of groups and organisations) theory. The background reading to this course is written up in the book *Group Approaches in Psychiatry* (Whiteley and Gordon, 1979).

In this and similar ways there was a sustained attempt to bring Henderson back within the field of general psychiatry into the present decade by cultivating more teaching contacts with other hospitals and the various post-graduate courses and generally espousing a less anti-psychiatry attitude. Nevertheless, although interest in Henderson remains keen, a research enquiry (Manning and Rapoport, 1976) showed that few psychiatrists actually wished to work there.

Rosow (one of the Rapoport team) had noted that, in the innovative years, referral to Henderson tended to come from doctors who had just visited or were from one of the major teaching centres and that these fell off as the doctors concerned moved into mainstream posts.  In the late 60's and 70's it has seemed that referrals come from a steady group of devotees dotted all over the country, few from the teaching centres and that there remain those antipathetic to the method as well as those sympathetic.

Criminological research and publications have resulted in Henderson once more being regarded as a special resource in the treatment of psychopaths as the many invited papers and lectures show.  Whiteley was asked to participate in the NATO Advanced Study Institute on Psychopathic Behaviour (1973) to contribute to the Broadmoor Symposium (1979) on Dangerousness with a reference to the psychopath and he is a regular lecturer on a number of Forensic Psychiatry courses on this subject.  He was called in a Chairman of a Working Party on the Management of Disturbed and Aggressive Patients by the Merton, Sutton and Wandsworth AHA (Wandsworth and East Merton Teaching District) in 1975.

The training influence of Henderson has extended into many penal institutions directly or indirectly.  Barrett, a former psychiatrist at Henderson has gone on to become Clinical Director at Grendon Underwood and has revived the training link for prison officers.

Similarly, prison officers from Barlinnie Prison in Glasgow came down to Henderson to develop ideas and plans for the Special Unit (a therapeutic community) for the most difficult prisoners in that institution.

Approximately 30 students come each year to spend placements of two weeks to six months at Henderson.  They are mostly social work students but include nursing, probation, psychology and medical students from a wide variety of Universities and Colleges.  Staff and patients from Henderson conduct seminars at a number of other hospitals or social work colleges whilst staff teams or lecturers are in demand at conferences  or on training courses.

Peper Harrow, formerly an Approved School for delinquent adolescent boys, took on a former Henderson psychiatrist as consultant and moved toward the Henderson therapeutic community model.  A former probation officer at Henderson, Bruce Pearce, in consultation with Henderson staff, set up the Surrey Community Development Trust hostels to cater for inadequate offenders in the Henderson way.  The idea was to set up a range of therapeutic communities offering differing degrees of control and care as appropriate in the way that the Henderson research had indicated.

Currently, Henderson staff are utilising their skills in the treatment of youngsters excluded from local schools as trouble-makers by involving them in activity groups.

Manor and O'Brien have obtained Ph.D's through psychological and sociological studies of the Henderson Community and this unique population of largely psychopathic offenders - voluntarily in treatment - continues to provide subjects for a number of current research projects.

The obscure problem of the physiological responsiveness of psychopaths is being investigated[3] (shades of the Effort Syndrome Unit); changes in self-esteem and attitudes to authority are being compared with such in a group of young offenders in a Detention Centre and in an after-care hostel;[4] and the different response of the different psychological types to therapeutic community treatment is being monitored in a long-term follow-up.

In the present closure crisis a gratifying result has been the volume of support and testimony that has come in from the UK and abroad. Scandinavians have stressed the importance of Henderson in social work training. Centres in the USA and Netherlands have acknowledged their respect for both the early and continued work at Henderson.

From the UK the support has emphasised two major themes. On the one hand there has been a strong body of evidence from consultant colleagues who recognise the Henderson as the treatment centre for patients too difficult to cope with in an orthodox psychiatric hospital. They emphasise that these patients need exposure to the confrontative peer group as a learning situation. The strongest lobby of support has come from the forensic psychiatrists who have described Henderson as being the model for the hospital-based (Secure Unit) treatment of mentally abnormal offenders. Probation officers, in particular, affirm the Henderson as the place where the difficult offender with the complication of an emotional disorder may be treated whilst social work agencies and tutors have stressed the value of the "living and learning" experience for students of social psychiatry.

Thus, out of it all comes the picture of Henderson as having developed (1) a particular sociotherapeutic model of a therapeutic community and (2)

---

[3] Now published by Gudjonsson and Roberts (1985) cited in the annotated bibliography.

[4] Now published by Norris (1983) cited in the annotated bibliography.

found its special role in the treatment of the personality disordered patient as the primary task. The present closure threat and the resultant response from the caring professions has told us better than any solicited review might have done just what a unique influence Henderson has had in psychiatry over the past 30 years.

## REFERENCES

COPAS, J. & WHITELEY, J.S. (1976)   Predicting success in the treatment of psychopaths. *British Journal of Psychiatry* 129, pp 388-392.

EAST, N. & HUBERT, W. (1939)   *The psychological treatment of crime*   London, H.M.S.O.

EDELSON, M. (1970) *Sociotherapy and psychotherapy.*   Chicago: University of Chicago Press.

HENDERSON, D.K. (1939) *Psychopathic states*, London: Chapman and Hall.

JONES, M. (1942) Group psychotherapy. *British Medical Journal*, 2, pp 276-278.

JONES, M. (1949) Acting as an aid to therapy in a neurosis centre. *British Medical Journal*, 1, pp 756-761.

JONES, M. (1962) *Social psychiatry in the community, in hospitals, and in prisons.* Springfield, Illinois: Charles C Thomas Publications.

JONES, M. (1968) *Beyond the therapeutic community*   New Haven: Yale University Press.

JONES, M., BAKER, A, FREEMAN, T., et al.(1952)   *Social psychiatry: A study of therapeutic communities.*   London: Tavistock Publishers.

JONES, M. & RAPOPORT, R. (1955)   Administrative and social psychiatry.   *Lancet*, 2, p 386.

KREEGER, L. (1975) *The large group*   London: Constable.

MANNING, N. (1976)a Innovation in social policy: The case of the therapeutic community. *Journal of Social Policy*, 5(3), pp 265-279.

MANNING, N. (1976)b Values and practice in the therapeutic community. *Human Relations*, 29 (2), pp 125-138..

MANNING, N. & RAPOPORT, R.(1976)   Rejection and re-incorporation: A case study in social research utilisation. *Social Science & Medicine*, 10, pp 459-468.

MANOR, O. (1979) *Social roles and behavioural change.*   Ph.D. Thesis, University of London.

MOOS, R.M. (1974) *Evaluating treatment environments.*   New York: John Wiley.

O'BRIEN, M. (1976) *Psychopathic disorder.*   Ph.D. Thesis, University of London.

RAPOPORT, R. (1960)   *Community as doctor.*   London: Tavistock Publishers.

SMITH, B. (1966) Psychopaths - Permissiveness or restriction. *Occupational Therapy.* November, pp 19-23.

STANTON, A.H. & SCHWARTZ, MS (1954) *The mental hospital.* New York: Basic Books.

WHITAKER, D.S. & LEIBERMAN, M.A. (1965) *Psychotherapy through the group process.* London: Tavistock Publishers.

WHITELEY, J.S. (1970) The response of psychopaths to a therapeutic community. *British Journal of Psychiatry,* 116, pp 534-529.

WHITELEY, J.S. (1978) The dilemmas of leadership in the therapeutic community and the large group. *Group Analysis,* 11(1), pp 40-47.

WHITELEY, J.S. (1979) The psychiatric hospital as a therapeutic setting. In P Righton (Ed.). *Studies in environment therapy* (Vol. 3). Toddington: The Planned Environment Therapy Trust.

WHITELEY, J.S. & ZLATIC, M. (1972) A re-appraisal of staff attitudes to the therapeutic community. *British Journal of Social Psychiatry,* 3, (2); pp 76-81.

# Personality Disordered Individuals:
## The Henderson Hospital Model of Treatment

Kingsley Norton

*Criminal Behaviour and Mental Health,*
*1992, Vol. 2 (2): pp 80-191*

The existence of hospitals social services and penal systems, reflects society's attempts to exert care, control and punishment over itself. The internal organisation and operation of these institutions also reflect society's wider attitudes, its prevailing philosophies and value systems, towards its sick, mad and bad members. However, the internal organisation and operation of institutions is also fashioned by its staff, its clientele and their inevitable interaction (Manning, 1980; Hinshelwood, 1987). Both external and internal influences exert an effect on a given institution, thus the internal structure and functioning of institutions is the result of dynamic, interactive processes.

## THE SHAPING OF AN INSTITUTION

Henderson Hospital was set up after World War II to aid the resettlement of servicemen. Its first Medical Director, Maxwell Jones, in his work on 'effort syndrome', had witnessed how much patients could educate and help fellow patients, particularly in group discussions. This observation was put to practical use and developed further within the unit. An internal re-organisation of the traditional hospital structures, incorporating the changed status of patients led to a hospital unit whose treatment approach moved away from an authoritarian, hierarchical style to one which was more collaborative and democratic - a 'therapeutic community' (Main, 1946).

Patients were *expected* to take an active part both in their own treatment and also that of other patients. The traditional hierarchy between doctor/nurse/patient became less rigid; there was more open communication among staff and patients and this was facilitated by daily discussion of the whole unit, comprising all its sub-groups (Jones, 1952).

The result is an institution, run as a therapeutic community, catering for adults, between the ages of 17 and 45 (Whiteley, 1980). Most suffer from personality disorder and derive from a segment of the difficult and offender patient category.

Henderson, as an institution, is in the unusual position of having developed *self-consciously* with the active participation of its client group in its internal organisation and operation. Therefore its study may provide information which indicates some of the treatment needs of the particular client group and also some of the ways in which such needs can be met. Research findings have indicated that both personal distress (Dolan, Wilson and Evans, 1992) and re-conviction/re-hospitalisation rates (Whiteley, 1970; Copas and Whiteley, 1976) improve substantially from Henderson Hospital treatment in approximately fifty per cent of cases.

## DESCRIPTIVE CHARACTERISTICS OF HENDERSON HOSPITAL RESIDENTS

Before considering what characterises Henderson's structure and function, it is important to define the client group which has influenced its development. Figures 1 and 2 show selected sociodemographic and other relevant historical (especially forensic) profiles of patients based on 46 admissions in 1990. The group can be broadly described as personality disordered. Sub-categories of the diagnostic group of personality disorders hold little meaning because of the large amount of personality disorder co-morbidity found in such populations. Coid (1990), for example, found that patients in a maximum security setting displayed personality disorder co-morbidity with women showing, on average, three and men, on average, two personality disorder diagnoses. In recent work at Henderson, using the self-rating Personality Disorder Questionnaire (Hyler, and Ryder, 1987), men averaged 7.2 (S.D. = 2.6) and women averaged 6.7) S.D. = 2.5) DSM-III-R Axis II diagnoses (Dolan, Evans and Norton, 1992). Of the twenty-four patients

FIGURE 1:  Characteristics of admissions to Henderson Hospital

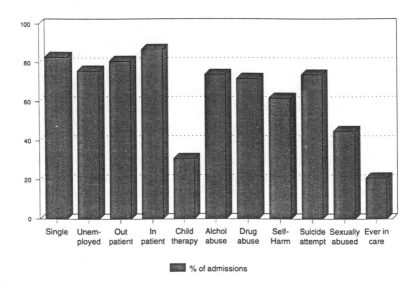

FIGURE 2:  Forensic profile of admissions

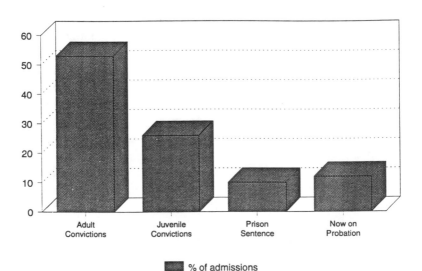

who took part in our pilot study, only one had a single personality disorder diagnosis (borderline personality disorder) and another individual patient had ten of the eleven DSM-III-R Axis II diagnoses tested for. Henderson clients' diagnoses are mostly (96 per cent) classifiable into Cluster B, the dramatic, erratic group of personality disorders of DSM-III-R (as opposed to 83% and 79% for Clusters A and C respectively).[1]

## ENGAGEMENT IN THERAPY

Regardless of treatment method or setting, regular difficulties are encountered in treating such patients. Problems centre on meaningful engagement and maintenance in therapy. A feature of the Henderson Hospital model is that therapy is voluntary. Thus it is never a condition of a criminal disposal and residents are not admitted under Sections of the Mental Health Act (1983).

Nurturing engagement is a paramount concern and the process of engagement begins at selection interview. As with all Henderson activities, selection is made in a group setting by residents and staff together, an example of "communalism" (Rapoport, 1960). Residents out-number staff by 3 : 1 in the selection group. Four candidates for admission are invited to each selection group interview and are interviewed, sequentially, by the group. Candidates are invited to talk about themselves as people; their current and past difficulties; previous treatment received; aspects of their childhood and adolescence, and asked what problems they would wish to address if admitted to Henderson. Notes relating to the interviews are taken by one resident and one staff member. The residents' record of the interview is presented to the whole community prior to a successful candidate's admission.

After the formal group interview, there is a closed discussion, by staff and residents, of the candidates. This culminates in a democratic vote, by residents and staff, for and against admission of each candidate. Residents can readily out-vote staff and thus they have the major say in who is admitted, an example of "democratisation" (Rapoport, 1960).

---

[1]   More detailed information on multiple diagnoses of personality disorder is given in the study by Dolan, Evans and Norton (1995). See annotated bibliography.

Of the residents, only the more senior (longer than three months' stay) are involved in the selection process, which itself is an important ingredient of their own treatment. During the selection group, these residents experience the weight of decision making, being on the "authority" end of the transaction, for a change. Residents see themselves and their difficulties reflected in the candidates who come for admission and they begin to realise how they appear to others or, at least, how they used to appear. Residents also experience some empowerment in making a decision regarding another person, which might be highly influential for that person's future. Heated discussion often results over whether to admit, particularly when there are issues of sexual victimisation; physical violence; arson; homosexuality or racial prejudice (Dolan, Polley, Allen and Norton, 1991).

Research into the selection process using SCL-90R (Derogatis, Lipman and Covi, 1973), has shown that those not selected (approximately one third of candidates interviewed) tend to be more somatising, obsessive/compulsive and phobic in their symptomatology (Dolan, Morton and Wilson, 1990). It appears, therefore, that the selection group is picking, among other attributes, those who have a capacity to verbalise feelings and psychosocial difficulties and to function in a group setting. The latter is important since all therapy at Henderson is group based, from the daily community meeting (involving all residents and staff); through the small group psychotherapy (thrice weekly) to art therapy, psychodrama (both weekly events) and the task-centred work groups (cookery, gardening and maintenance and artwork twice weekly). The resident's weekly programme is shown in figure 3.

Even when meaningful engagement has been established, remaining in treatment long enough to make lasting personality change is problematical. At Henderson maintenance of engagement is facilitated via the effect of a variety of features of the hospital's internal organisation and operation, resulting in a therapeutic mixture of supportive containment and reality confrontation, (Rapoport, 1960).

*Formal patient hierarchy*
The resident group, as a whole, is deliberately hierarchically structured, with respect to elected positions or jobs within the community which residents hold for a month at a time. Changing of post-holders means that residents

FIGURE 3:  The Residents' Programme.

| | MONDAY | TUESDAY | WEDNESDAY | THURSDAY | FRIDAY | SAT. | SUN. |
|---|---|---|---|---|---|---|---|
| 9.15-10.30 | "9.15" Community Meeting | | | | | Free Time | |
| 10.30-11.00 | Morning Break | | | | | | |
| 11.00-12.00 | Small Group Psychotherapy | Reviews & Cleaning Elections or Community Projects | Small Group Psychotherapy or Leavers' Group | Welfare Group Probation Group or Visitors Group | Small Group Psychotherapy | | |
| 12.00-13.30 | Lunch Break | | | | | | |
| 13.30-14.00 | Surgery | | Cleaning | | | | |
| 14.15 or 14.30-16.30 | Psychodrama or Art Therapy | Selection, Community Work Group or Housing Group | Art Therapy or Psychodrama | Gardening & Maintenance, Art Work Group or Welfare Group | | | |
| 16.45-17.00 | Floor Meeting | | | | | | |
| 17.00-17.15 | 'Handover' to night staff (Two residents & two day staff) | | | | | | |
| 18.00-19.00 | | Women's Group | | Men's Group | | | |
| 19.00-21.00 | COMMUNITY MEAL | | | | | | |
| 21.15-22.05 | "Tens" Group (optional) | | | | | 'Tens' | |
| 22.15-23.00 | Summit Meeting (Top three residents and staff) | | | | | | |
| 23.00 | Night Round (Top three residents and staff) | | | | | | |

gain experience of being on each end of a responsibility spectrum. The posts relate to real tasks (as opposed to activities designed solely to occupy time) which need to be carried out for the internal running of the Unit both within unstructured time and the formal treatment programme. The accent is on how the task is undertaken, on "means" rather then "ends" (Norton, 1990).

The community is headed by the "Top Three" residents who are supported by a fourth, the "General Secretary". These four residents, who have to have been resident for at least three months in order to be nominated to their positions, co-ordinate the day-to-day community activities during their one month's tenure. This includes setting the agenda for the day's community meeting, (at an 11 p.m. meeting, called the "Summit", the previous evening); chairing the daily community meeting; leading the weekly selection group; and deciding when to call emergency meetings of the community.

Other elected posts are open to residents on the basis of length of stay and include: the keeping of attendance registers at therapy groups; cooking and storage of food and devising cleaning rotas. There are sufficient jobs for all residents. Elections to posts take place monthly and only residents are able to vote; staff, however, participate in the discussions prior to the voting.

One of the larger gaps between levels in the residents' hierarchical organisation is that between "new" residents and the remainder. Initially, "new" residents have a three week induction, including their own small group, and enjoy a privileged position by virtue of being excused cleaning duties during their first week. However, there is a debit side to this in that "new" residents are not allowed to vote in the first week and are therefore more to be seen than heard in the community! The "new" resident may test the position in the pecking order, often via rule-breaking. This will provide him/her with an insight into how the rules of the community are implemented (see below). One effect of the hierarchical organisation is that residents know where they stand in the formal hierarchy and, overall, this can facilitate a feeling of security or containment.

*Rigid timetable*
Containment is also effected by the programme of the community which is rigidly organised with fixed time boundaries, strictly adhered to, albeit with fixed periods of lee-way. Thus ten minutes absence from a therapy group is

the maximum which is tolerated by the community before the group is officially missed. This fact is then routinely announced at the next day's community meeting, under one of the standing items of the agenda, and the resident in question needs to account for the absence. Missing more than two therapy groups in one week means that all groups the next day must be attended in full. At the end of this, a treatability vote is taken by the whole community. Again, residents' greater numbers mean that they have greater power than staff to decide on who leaves and when. The resident in question may be discharged from the community unless an adequate reason, show of remorse or good intentions for the future is demonstrated and accepted. Given that re-admission is unlikely, discharge is the ultimate censure but this power depends on the resident being sufficiently engaged with the community.

There are two points to make here. Firstly, residents know they are expected to be in certain places at certain times, that their absence will be noted and they will be called to account over this. Secondly, rules are implemented so as to encourage residents to reflect on why a rule, for example missing groups, has been broken - again an accent on "means" rather than "ends". This facilitates building up of a cause-effect type of thinking (including psychological mindedness); "thinking before acting" and taking into account the effect actions have on others.

Those who are not prematurely discharged become increasingly attached to the community and its members. Because of the variety in the structured programme and the large amount of social contact that takes place in the domestic and the unstructured time (including during the undertaking of domestic duties), there are many niches into which individual residents may fit with a beneficial impact on self-esteem (Norris, 1983). Some demand more verbal skills and others more practical or manual ones.

*Rules: breaking and enforcing*
Breaking rules, to do with proscribing violence (to self, others and property) and illicit drugs or alcohol intake, occasion automatic discharge. Such rule-breakers are considered by the community to have discharged themselves, but may ask for permission to stay until the community meets in full the following morning (an example of "permissiveness", i.e. tolerance of greater

deviance than is normal in society at large (Rapoport, 1960)). Assuming concensus permission is granted (following discussion, at an emergency meeting) then the miscreant has to attend all groups the following day and then undergo a "readmission" vote.

It is, perhaps, surprising that enforcing the community's rules at Henderson is relatively easy. The major reason is that the residents themselves enforce rules, having been on the receiving end of intoxicated, disordered, violent, neglectful or abusing others previously (i.e. rule breakers). Rule enforcement by residents gives power to people who have often been disempowered victims. The tendency is towards a harsh, unempathic and unthinking rule enforcement and at times staff need to act to mitigate this effect.

*Community meeting*
The morning (Monday to Saturday) community meeting is central since it is a forum for all residents and all staff on duty to meet and to discuss matters of relevance to the running of the community. The meeting has a number of standing items as well as an open part of the agenda. It is chaired, in rotation, by the "Top Three" residents. Missing the community meeting, or more than ten minutes of it has the same consequences as described for the therapy groups.

The meeting deals with most of the day-to-day administrative and domestic activities associated with running the community. At a given item on the agenda, staff are invited to feedback matters such as annual leave; writing of reports; nursing or medical matters, Residents' minutes are presented from a "wind-down" meeting, which is held each evening at 10 p.m., for those who for one reason or another are finding it difficult to settle for the night. Matters arising, together with any other topics discussed by "Top Three", as being of importance to the community at the time, appear as standing items on the next morning's agenda. In this way topical issues, for example, upset after a resident has been discharged by the community (which otherwise might be ignored or denied), are brought to the attention of the community as a whole. Personality clashes or other problems between residents or between residents and staff are discussed and potentially resolved in this setting. The meeting serves many important functions: enhancing cohesion and a feeling of belonging to the community; alerting attention to distressed members and executing an examination of rule-breaking behaviour. Most of the "votes" are carried out in this setting (see above).

*Response to serious incidents or distress*
Having become engaged in treatment, residents struggle to keep to the rules of the community but inevitably these get broken. If an important rule (for example, one occasioning automatic discharge) has been broken, or a resident is particularly distressed, then the "Top Three" residents will call an emergency meeting at any time of day or night. All community members must attend (or else be on a discharge vote themselves). The various resources of the community may be mobilised in order to support the resident in question. At night this may entail others sleeping in or outside the individual's bedroom or, a number of residents, together with the distressed one, occupying a larger room. Staff who also attend the emergency meetings do not otherwise participate in providing this practical help. No psychotropic medication is ever prescribed.

There is much emotional and practical support in the community for those residents viewed as deserving and especially for those who have previously provided such support for others or who are viewed as genuinely tackling their problems. Tolerance, however, is limited and this fact can be beneficial, often resulting in confrontation if the distressed role is overplayed and tips into an act of manipulation. If fellow residents have repeatedly sat up with you, through the night, they will not be pleased if you do not begin to chase your deviant ways of expressing distress and start to use the therapy groups during daylight hours! Thus, compared to many other settings, deviant behaviour (as a way of expressing otherwise unbearable psychic pain) is not reinforced but genuine struggling with emotion is. There is no "specialling" by staff and therefore no endless supply of one-to-one relationships, which can tend to reinforce sick, or manipulative, behaviour.

*Disengaging*
For those who stay, Henderson has often become a place of special attachment and security and leaving is difficult. For some residents, in the past, leaving has been synonymous with expulsion and often the community

will be set up by a resident perhaps by rule-breaking in order for this pattern to be repeated. Once this strategy is seen through, however, the resident is supported, encouraged, cajoled or shamed into owning his or her feelings in the face of leaving. Aggression is often an easier emotion to tolerate than sadness and also a camouflage for it. Repeated working through is necessary if the resident is to "leave properly" (Wilson, 1985).

Nobody at Henderson seems quite sure what "leaving properly" means although the phrase is liberally used and, sometimes, wielded as a stick with which to beat the resident into owning feelings of sadness. "Leaving properly" certainly requires that some degree of planning take place. Ideally, the community is also in agreement that the resident has achieved what is feasible by this stage. In order to facilitate this there is a "leavers'" group, which takes place weekly during small group time. Both practical and emotional issues are explored and hopefully resolved in this setting. Just as the new residents have their own small group for the first three weeks, which involves a senior resident, so the "leavers'" group involves a non-leaving resident. Information from this group is regularly fed back into the community meeting.

The maximum stay at the Henderson is one year. There is no formal follow-up treatment,[2] although currently there is a follow-up research study in place. The absence of follow-up treatment reflects the lack of resources; low exit rates; wide (national) catchment area; group treatments and the importance of working through the leaving process itself. If, for example, individual psychotherapy were available automatically post-discharge, this would inevitably have an effect on the emotional process of leaving and the resident's ability to work it through. However, prior to discharge, many residents will set up supportive social structures for themselves, sometimes incorporating further psychotherapy.

---

[2]   Although this was true at the time of writing, in 1995 Henderson established an Outreach Service which provides both follow-up support for ex-residents and an out-patient treatment and consultation service for other personality disordered clients.

## ROLE OF STAFF

There is insufficient space to discuss the staff structures and their function in detail. The staff team (approximately 25 w.t.e.) is multi-disciplinary; uniforms are not worn and first names are used. There is the well known "flattened hierarchy" and much "blurring of roles", with nursing staff and social therapists much more involved in treatment than in traditional psychiatric settings. Individual staff do take responsibility for particular aspects of community life. Importantly, continuity of staff among the various therapy groups is maintained, as far as possible. There are no distinct night staff and most staff (nine charge nurses, three staff nurses and six social therapists) work shifts and the remainder (three whole-time equivalent medical staff, senior nurse manager, social worker, art therapist and research psychologist) work 9 a.m-5 p.m., Monday to Friday. At night, and at weekends, there are only two staff on duty, except for the Saturday morning community meeting which is also attended by one of the medical staff.

There are daily multidisciplinary staff meetings which take place at morning handover and at lunchtime. Handover from day staff to night staff, in the evening, also involves residents. Staff meet after all the main treatment groups to review what has taken place. There are also staff meetings which deal with business matters; with mutual supervision of clinical work (weekly) and there is a fortnightly academic meeting. The weekly staff sensitivity group is facilitated by an outside psychotherapist and is set up to deal with staff-staff conflicts as they might relate to the professional context.

All staff meetings take place in group settings and the flattened hierarchy means that decision-making about the unit's business and internal management matters is via negotiation and consensus. In this way staff are kept in touch with the reality of having to function as a group of more or less equals (despite obvious hierarchical aspects and differences). To an extent, this situation mirrors that of the residents. The staff's working day is even more highly structured than that of the residents. Resultant time pressures, together with the group setting, facilitate an empathic understanding of the residents' experience of being in the community. This is important since maintaining empathic contact with such a client group is not easy.

## RELEVANCE OF THE HENDERSON HOSPITAL METHOD TO OTHER SETTINGS

Henderson's treatment method evolved, and continues to evolve, under the influence of its particular clientele. It cannot claim, necessarily, any wider application. However, some ingredients of the treatment method may be generalisable and of use in other settings. The following are offered as treatment ingredients for personality disordered individuals which may generalise:

(1) *Participation of patients in an authentic negotiation of their own treatment goals and involvement in the treatment of fellow patients.* Although this may be difficult to achieve in more secure settings than Henderson, without doubt there are ways in which progress can be made towards greater participation.   This should include collaborative involvement with staff in the day to day running of ward activities.  For this to happen it is important to have personality disordered patients under one roof and to meet formally and regularly, together with staff, in a large group (community) setting. This means that the given institution has to confront any fears engendered by such an idea and be generally supportive of such a development.  Among patients with heterogenous diagnoses, a small number of personality disordered patients can be seriously detrimental to overall function of the ward (Miller, 1989).

(2) *A range of environments which support changing hierarchical organisations of patients is required* Groups of individuals living together tend to structure and organise themselves via hierarchies. In hospitals, such structures can be more or less democratic and respectful of their members (Winnicott, 1950; Kennard, 1989). Although the role of the staff in maintaining an humane structure is crucial, the culture tends to be passed on, importantly, by those patients more senior and/or powerful in it. Patients need to be able to experience being both higher up and lower down the "official" patient hierarchy.

Within a given "community" there needs to be a sufficient flow of patients through it so that malignant or fixed structures are minimised. These come about if too many senior patients are forced to remain in an environment which can no longer sustain their continued emotional and social development. Necessarily exploitative means of survival are found by a group of personality disordered patients under such conditions. Patients who are genuinely developing, therefore, need to move through a range of treatment settings of appropriate sophistication, ultimately, leading to discharge. A comprehensive range of facilities, therefore, is required to enable the successful patient, who manages personality maturation within a secure setting, to maintain therapeutic momentum.

(3) To engage patients in their own treatment and that of their peers, the ward environment must be able to support changing hierarchical patient structures. This requires *staff structures* which are *sufficiently flexible* and *which avoid overly hierarchical and authoritarian styles*. The Henderson Hospital staff structures already described, albeit briefly, indicate one model.

# REFERENCES

COPAS, J.B. and WHITELEY, J.S. (1976) Predicting success in the treatment of psychopaths. *British Journal of Psychiatry.* 129, pp 388-392.

COID, J.N. (1989) Psychopathic disorders. *Current Opinions in Psychiatry,* 2, pp 750-756.

DEROGATIS, L.R., LIPMAN, R.S. and COVI, L. (1973) SCL-90: An outpatient psychiatric rating scale preliminary report. *Psychopharmacology Bulletin,* 9(1), pp 13-28.

DOLAN, B., MORTON, A. and WILSON, J. (1990) Selection of admissions to a therapeutic community using a group setting association with degree and type of psychological distress. *International Journal of Social Psychiatry* 36 (4), pp 265-271.

DOLAN B, EVANS C.D.H., NORTON K. (1992) The separation individuation inventory: Association with borderline pphenomena. *Journal of Nervous and Mental Disease.* 180 (8); pp 529-533.

DOLAN B.M., EVANS C.D.H., and WILSON J. (1992) Therapeutic Community treatment for personality disordered adults: Changes in neurotic symptomatology on follow-up *International Journal of Social Psychiatry* Vol. 38 (4) pp 243-250

DOLAN, B., POLLEY, K., ALLEN, R. and NORTON, M. (1991) Addressing racism in psychiatry: Is the therapeutic community model applicable? *International Journal of Social Psychiatry* 37(2), pp 71-79.

HINSHELWOOD, R.D. (1987) *What happens in groups: psychoanalysis, the individual and the community*: London, Free Association Books.

JONES, M. (1952) *Social Psychiatry*. London: Tavistock Publications.

KENNARD, D. (1989) The therapeutic impulse: what makes it grow? *International. Journal of Therapeutic Communities* 10, (3) pp 155-163.

MAIN, T. (1946) The hospital as a therapeutic institution. *Bulletin of the Menninger Clinic* 10, pp 66-68.

MANNING, N. (1980) Collective disturbance in institutions: a sociological view of crisis and collapse. *International Journal of Therapeutic Communities* 1, pp 147-158.

MILLER, L.J. (1989) In-patient management of borderline personality disorder: a review and update  *Journal of Personality. Disorder*, 3(2), pp 122-124.

NORRIS, M. (1983) Changes in patients during treatment at Henderson Hospital therapeutic community during 1977-1981. *British Journal of Medical Psychology* 56, pp 135-143.

NORTON, K. (1991) The significance and importance of the therapeutic community working practice. *International Journal of Therapeutic Communities* 11 (2), pp 67-76.

RAPOPORT, R. (1960) *The community as doctor*. London: Tavistock Publications.

WHITELEY, J.S. (1970) The response of psychopaths to a therapeutic community. *British Journal of Psychiatry* 116, pp 517-529.

WHITELEY, J.S. (1980) The Henderson Hospital. *International Journal of Therapeutic Communities* 1 (1) , pp 38-58.

WILSON, J. (1985) Leaving home as a theme in a therapeutic community. *International Journal of Therapeutic Communities*  6 (2), pp 71-78.

WINNICOTT, D.W. (1950) Some thoughts on the meaning of the word Democracy. Republished in: *Home is where we start from*. Harmondsworth: Pelican.


## ACKNOWLEDGEMENTS

*Figures 1 and 2 are reproduced courtesy of Dr. Bridget Dolan who also made helpful comments on the text. Figure 3 is taken from promotional material produced by Henderson staff and residents*

# A Culture of Enquiry:
# Its Preservation or Loss

Kingsley Norton

*International Journal of Therapeutic Communities*
*(1992) Vol. 13(1), pp 3-25*

This paper examines certain of Main's contributions to therapeutic community theory and practice using Henderson Hospital as an example. Main's concept of a "culture of enquiry" is amplified. Culture and structure are described in their interaction and in their combined effect to produce therapeutic change. Ways in which a therapeutic culture can be lost, in the short and long-term, are discussed. It is argued that the responsibility for preserving a "culture of enquiry" rests mainly with the staff. Through meeting in group settings, staff, like resident members of the community, are exposed to regressive pulls into immature modes of expression and resolution of personal and interpersonal conflict.

## INTRODUCTION

In discussing the concept of the therapeutic community, Main (1983) argued that it is "not the structure but the culture which is decisive for the human relations on offer". In the same paper, he referred to the therapeutic community as a "culture of enquiry .... into personal and interpersonal and inter-system problems and a study of impulses, defences and relations as these are expressed and arranged socially". The aim of the present paper is threefold. Firstly, to amplify Main's "definition" of a therapeutic community, with reference to Henderson Hospital (see Whiteley, (1980) for details of history and development of this therapeutic community) and, in particular, to develop an understanding of the phrase "culture of enquiry". Secondly, to consider the interactive relationship between structure and culture and thereby to attempt to explain how therapeutic change is effected via the combination of structure and culture. Thirdly, since a therapeutic culture implies a more or less stable situation, to discuss ways in which it may be de-stabilised or lost, both in the short-term and long-term, so that only a devitalised, non-therapeutic, structure remains.

The structure of an organisation refers to those aspects which impose constraints upon the behaviour of its members, limiting freedom of action and choice in a variety of situations. It does not prescribe, however, every form of behaviour which takes place within it (Glen, 1975). Although not dictating a particular culture, the structure of a therapeutic community exerts an influence on the type and quality of culture which can develop. Culture cannot exist in the absence of structure and there is no structure without a co-existing culture. Thus concepts of structure and culture are inextricably linked, perhaps, in an analogous way to those of the living brain and the mind.

Before examining the vicissitudes of Henderson Hospital's culture, its structure will be described. (There is not room to consider the physical structure and environment of Henderson Hospital in spite of the obvious relevance of such factors). The main components to be considered are as follows:   the clientele;   the selection of residents;   the therapeutic programme;   the formal hierarchy of the residents' sub-system;   the community's rules and the mechanism of enforcement;   and aspects of the staff subsystems' role and function.

The above components of the structure of Henderson Hospital represent, for the most part, formal aspects. As such they do not adequately define the total structure of the organisation, less still its culture. The latter reflects as much the informal processes which intermingle with and interact with the formal structures and contribute to the expression of culture at any given point in time (Manning, 1989). Necessarily, the informal aspects of the community are harder to describe since they are often only tacitly acknowledged to exist and their true extent and importance is only revealed once they are lost or significantly disturbed.

## HENDERSON HOSPITAL "STRUCTURE"

*Clientele*
The client group of Henderson has been described in detail elsewhere (Whiteley, 1970). Commensurate with their active participation in their own

and others' treatment they are not referred to as patients, but as "residents". Henderson Hospital residents have in common a similar level of personality organisation, namely, borderline (Kernberg, 1976). However, they comprise, broadly, two categories. One is typified by a tendency to "act" and the other by a tendency to "retreat". Such habitual strategies are deployed in response to emotional conflict otherwise intolerable and inexpressible and exert an effect of temporary diffusion of psychic discomfort and pain.

Diagnostically, clients come under the category of personality disorder (W.H.O., 1978; A.P.A., 1980). Sub-categories of personality disorder diagnosis are unreliable especially in client populations, such as at Henderson, where the condition is more severe (Coid, 1990; Grove and Tellegen, 1991). Borderline personality disorder is the most common diagnosis (Dolan et al., 1992). Henderson Hospital's residents show moderate to severe personality disorder, although severity is difficult to reliably measure.

In a detailed psychological study, O'Brien (1976) identified four major types of patient at Henderson: the anxious intropunitive (neurotic), anxiety-free extrapunitive (psychopathic), anxious extrapunitive and anxiety-free intropunitive. However, Figures 1 and 2 (see page 33) show some of the important socio-demographic and clinical characteristics of the Henderson Hospital therapeutic community residents viewed at a single point in time. This introduces another method of describing the client group and provides a kind of snap-shot of the community, which may convey a more vivid clinical picture of residents than does either a description of overall personality organisation, a consideration of personality disorder diagnostic sub-categories or other psychological profile.

*Impact of admission*
Potentially, the effect of admission to Henderson is to reinstate the individual's emotional conflict, albeit within an emotional and physical environment which supports the development and application of new, less extreme and less maladaptive, strategies. The mechanism for the constellation of conflict differs for the two categories of resident. Those who habitually "act" are bound by the rules, particularly no violence to self, others or property. Those who habitually "retreat" must become involved in the formal activities of the community which are all group-based. They must attend the treatment programme with, for them, the risks and pressures consonant upon engaging in social interaction.

At the personal  level (Main, 1983), the result is residents who are in a state of inner tension generated by the requirement that they forego their usual means of dealing with conflict. At the interpersonal level (Main, 1983), among others, those residents who "act" are confronted by others who do likewise; whilst those who "retreat" are similarly faced with others who utilise avoidant defensive strategies. Those who "act" are also exposed to those who "retreat" and vice versa. The result is not only a potential for interpersonal learning (Yalom, 1975) but also for rivalry, competition and strife, resulting in an increased likelihood of resorting to usual defensive strategies. If the temptation to succumb to the impulse can be resisted, then, consequent upon developing a capacity to experience  the emotional conflict (for example,  feeling fearful, angry or depressed), there is the possibility of establishing more mature methods of adaptation and emotional expression.

At the level of intersystems (Main, 1983), there are myriad examples of pairing, sub-grouping and scapegoating which form and dissolve within the community. Many are transitory; they exist variously between residents and residents;  residents and staff;  and between staff and staff. Important among these are the relationship of the new to senior resident sub-systems and of the residents' sub-system, as a whole, to that of the staff. Some of the interactions which take place between these various sub-systems will be described later.

## THE INTER-RELATIONSHIP OF 'STRUCTURE' AND 'CULTURE'

The internal organisation and operation of an institution is shaped by its client group as well as by other factors, internal and external (Manning, 1980). Internally, the inevitable interaction between residents and staff has also helped to shape the institution (Kennard, 1979). Therefore, Henderson's structure has developed with an important contribution from its client group (Jones, 1952;   Norton, 1992). It bears an unmistakable, if imprecisely definable,  imprint of the client group, which has an important bearing on the stability of the organisation and the development and expression of its culture.

For Henderson's therapeutic community, as for any group-based treatment modality, there is the paradox of the "container" also being the "contained" (Zinkin, 1989). The fact that so many personality disordered residents can exert, under the particular and peculiar circumstances of the therapeutic community, a clearly demonstrable therapeutic effect (Whiteley,

1970; Copas and Whiteley, 1976; Dolan, et al., 1990) still surprises many health-care professionals. What requires explanation is how the particular organisation and its operation actually brings about change. The question can be framed, "How is a therapeutic culture ("culture of enquiry") set up and maintained?" There is no simple or single answer to this question.

*Culture expressed as meaningful ritual*
The whole treatment programme can be conceived as a single analytic session with staff involved in a continuous transference-countertransference situation (Whiteley, 1986). By its predictable time-space structuring the programme provides a "containing" function in respect of the residents' unintegrated or projected aspects as would the individual analytic session (Bion, 1961). Individual ingredients of the treatment programme subserve the same overall function and probably none more so than the daily community meeting, already described. Attending this meeting is something of a ritual activity and the wording used by the Chairperson is, at times, very precisely laid down and usually delivered without variation. Thus, each meeting starts with "Good morning .... Who's missing?". There follow other incantations, such as: "Groups and why?" (This translated means: "Who are those who have missed therapy groups so far this week and what are the reasons given by those who missed groups yesterday?").

Ritualism, as above, may have a therapeutic function (Usandivaras, 1985) but this begs the question of the mechanism by which this effect might be produced. Perera (1988) describes the importance of what she calls the analytic "ritual", specifically, for the containment and integration of aggression in borderline patients. She refers to ritual as, "a form of imaginative creativity .... serving as transition objects......". She views individual analysis as a ritual which permits both arousal and containment of aggression and sees containment as, "in part, involving the countering of aggression with another basic drive". The same can be said of the therapeutic community.

When such "countering of aggression with another basic drive" takes place, the effect on the individual is to constellate emotional conflict intrapersonally rather than interpersonally. Interpersonal conflict is often maintained by an automatic, unthinking retaliation, meeting like with like (Lambert, 1981). If this does not take place the individual in question is brought up sharp because of the absence of the expected retaliatory response from others. He or she is thus made (i.e. creatively enabled) to think or question. Something novel, or at least unusual, has taken place. What has resulted in such a circumstance is, in Perera's words, "a vision of acceptance rather than a battle" (Perera, 1988).

Two clinical examples follow. The first is close to what Perera (1988) described. The second is a clinical example of a male resident who expressed his aggression via flouting the rules, in this instance in connection with alcohol consumption and self-harm, and received over the course of a few months a variety of countering emotional responses from the community, especially as expressed during community meetings when his behaviour and motives were examined. The effect represented a depressive position (Klein, 1935) response on the part of the community rather than an apparently simpler countering of one "basic drive" with another.

## Clinical examples

- *Anna* was a dominant senior female resident who, in spite of a spindly androgynous appearance, for most of her stay displayed a hard, sarcastic, "macho" exterior. Brian was a newer, heavily intellectually defended, male resident who had little confidence and few friends within the community. At the time of the incident to be described both were members of Top Three.

  An alliance seemed to be forming between Anna and the third member of Top Three, who was a "macho" male with rigid views of right and wrong. Brian felt excluded and "summit" meetings became characterised by loud disagreements. When "summit discussed" was announced to the whole community as, "What is happening with Top Three?", a useful discussion ensued.

  Brian had tendered his resignation and he and the third member immediately entered on an unpleasant personalised and insulting dialogue. The rest of the community became involved with support being offered to each side. Anna was conspicuously silent until asked for her view. To the surprise of the community, but especially to Brian, she indicated that she had never liked him ("because of his philosophical crap") but, until he had tendered his resignation, she had begun to think that "underneath he (Brian) was a nice bloke".

- *Charles* was a male resident who had been at Henderson for eight months and had established a senior position in the community by being respected as somebody who spoke his mind and was generally considerate to, and supportive of other residents. He had been sexually abused by a family member, had left home prematurely in an unsatisfactory way and had led a drifting lifestyle with little intimate social contact; frequent change of (manual) jobs; much physical fighting and self-harming behaviour, especially when drunk. He had a significant alcohol dependence problem. He continued to have intermittent unsatisfactory contact with his parents (actually mother and stepfather). He tended to be valued at home only for the practical, handyman, tasks he could perform.

Initially, Charles had been a quiet member of the community, seemingly wanting, or hoping to fit in solely by making himself useful. Over a holiday period, away from the unit and its "structure", he had drunk (breaking one of the community's rules since he had not been given leave to drink alcohol by the community), overdosed and self-mutilated. The response of the community was muted but generally supportive, although most of the residents had been away at the time of the episode in question. To an extent, his actions appeared to draw Charles more into the mainstream of the community life.

Twice, later on in Charles' stay, there were further similar episodes. Each one, however, seemed to be less severe and he became more able to ask for help without resorting, so readily, to activity. As a result, the amount of self-harm was reduced. However, the community was asked, at his request, to sanction his control of his own drinking by giving their consent to his taking alcohol whilst off the unit in ordinary social situations. (This request came after he himself had been beaten up by three drunken men after an evening spent in a pub when he had remained "dry"). Not without much discussion, Charles was granted permission to take sole responsibility for his drinking.

Within a week, having experienced the community's "permission" as evidence of lack of caring, he had drunk alcohol and self-mutilated so severely that he required surgery to repair tendon damage and physiotherapy to prevent serious long-term loss of functioning. Whereas the first episode, referred to above, had met with little reaction from the community, the next two produced more anger and disappointment. This "final" episode, which had the greatest emotional impact on the community, seemed also to have maximal impact on Charles. It was as if for the first time he could really experience the emotional impact he had on others because they did genuinely care what happened to him. This had the effect of making him think. Many of the community's members were sad, angry, disappointed, sympathetic all at one and the same time. This contrasted very much with his mother's habitual response to him which was (maybe with some justification), "Trouble's back home again".

The reaction of the community to Charles' "final" episode had some of the hallmarks of a mature emotional response comprising, in its total effect, (and to varying degrees among the individual members of the community) a capacity to tolerate and express emotions which are often experienced as contradictory love/hate; sadness/anger;  sympathy/hostility hallmarks of the depressive position (Klein, 1935). Thus his paranoid-schizoid position anger was met with, in its collective effect, a depressive position response. However,  the community is not often able to sustain function of such a quality or  at such a mature level. Sometimes, for long periods, there prevails a tense or otherwise suspicious or hostile atmosphere, which seems to preclude such interchanges as above. An individual who, for example, self-harms during such periods, will be met with hostility or other negative reactions in more or less pure form, seemingly without regard to the individual's circumstances. What is going on at such times?

## LOSING A "CULTURE OF ENQUIRY"

Groups, and perhaps especially large groups (Hinshelwood and Gruneberg, 1979;  de Mare, 1985) display a tendency to function at what can be called an immature level basic assumption group (Bion, 1963). Under such circumstances the group, is, as if, in the grip of unconscious or irresistible forces impelling it to travel in any direction but that of the stated aim or purpose of the group. In a therapeutic community this implies non-therapeutic aims. Such basic assumption group functioning can happen in any group setting and, within a given group meeting it is possible to discern its appearance and disappearance.

There are many ways in which basic assumption group functioning is expressed but one particular mode, in the context of the Henderson community meeting, will be described. The particular clinical example relates to the idea of therapy as ritual, in the sense of meaningful or symbolic (depressive position) activity as opposed to rote rehearsal or recitation. Like ritual, the therapeutic culture  can be extinguished temporarily (c.f. basic assumption group functioning) within the duration of a given treatment session and, more importantly, can be extinguished over longer time frames in the context of the whole institution. Thus for a therapeutic culture to endure, the community's "cultural" ideas have to be embodied and expressed in an authentic manner and on a continuous basis (see Rapoport, 1960, for ideological themes of permissiveness; communalism; democratisation and reality confrontation).

Without an awareness that such ideas can lose their authentic meaning the risk is even greater that they will do so. If this happens, not only is the community temporarily deprived of therapeutic potential but also the future of the organisation itself is subtly threatened by the introduction of a discontinuity of its culture. A "culture of enquiry" implies a capacity to think and this is represented in the community, in part, by the achievement of a work group level of functioning (Bion, 1963). When this is displaced by basic assumption functioning, a capacity for mature thinking (for reflective thought with appropriate attendant emotion) is lost and along with it the potential for therapeutic change is diminished.

The following examples illustrate aspects of the relationship between work group and basic assumption group functioning; therapeutic culture and structure; and transforming as opposed to non-transforming activity in groups. They demonstrate the way in which the structure (specifically the potentially therapeutic "ritual" aspects of the community meetings) can be used defensively by the community to subvert the "culture of enquiry".

*Clinical Examples*
- In one community meeting the resident chairing the meeting said "Good-morning - who's-missing?". What is important here is the punctuation. In effect, the first two items of the agenda had been conflated. The meaning of "Good-morning" had been lost. This tiny fragment of the "ritual" of the whole community meeting, had lost its meaning. There was insufficient time for anybody to make a verbal response. Subsequently, there have been periods during which the meaning has returned and the structure been enlivened. Currently, however, there is a tendency for the community to chorus its reply of "good morning" and once more the authentic meaning has been lost.

- The second example, of a similar kind, concerns the topic discussed by the Top Three residents at their late night "summit" meeting (see earlier for terminology). The purpose is to inform the rest of the community what has been the preoccupation of the Top Three from the previous day's business. (This introduction of a topic serves an important function of continuity in the community's emotional life, linking events of the previous day to the feelings and thoughts of the present). The staff are already aware of the content of the previous evening's discussion from handover by night staff. On this particular occasion staff had been informed that the Top Three had discussed pertinent topics relating to the community's current concerns (at the time insecurity arising from staffing changes). However, Top Three, in effect, had stopped and begun to think afresh of a topic to introduce to the community rather than to record the essence of the actual discussion, to which the agenda item "Summit discussed" refers. This practice of Top Three became a trend. What was put on the agenda (for the period that "Summit discussed" had lost its meaning) was alternately bland or a theme considered to represent any topic which would be likely to stimulate a discussion.

Both of the above examples illustrate how aspects of the "structure" (these examples relate to fixed agenda items of the community) lose their potential capacity for "cultural" function once the meaning and thinking behind them is lost. As a result, fixed items on the agenda, and the language habitually heralding them, potentially part of a therapeutic ritual, become hollow sounding and exert little or no actual containing or transforming effect.

There are many other ways in which the "culture" of the therapeutic community can be lost but two further commonplace examples must suffice. The first involves the way in which "democratisation", as a key ideological theme (Rapoport, 1960), can be used defensively to block "thinking". What is enacted is democratic voting as a substitute for discussion (enquiry). The second example, to some extent similar and equally as common, demonstrates the way in which painful disagreement (which would otherwise necessitate seeing the other's point of view, hence also having to feel separate and, to an extent, dreadfully alone) is avoided.

*Clinical Examples*
- A female resident, Diana, had left the unit one lunchtime in the company of another female resident, having been distressed by a letter received

from her mother that morning. She proceeded, to the horror of her companion, to walk in front of passing traffic. Her companion was able to restrain her but since she could not persuade Diana to return to the Unit she herself rushed back for help from other residents. Help was forthcoming in the shape of four male residents who returned to the scene, which was close by. Together they were able to persuade her to return to Henderson.

An emergency meeting of the whole community was called since Diana's behaviour was construed as breaking the self-harm rule. The community agreed that this was indeed the case although no actual harm had resulted. As a result, Diana, who had in effect discharged herself by her behaviour, was required to ask for permission to stay on the Unit for twenty-four hours in order for the matter to be fully discussed and for an ensuing discharge vote to be taken regarding her future in the Unit. Without real conviction, Diana asked for permission to stay on. Rather than discuss the event and permit other residents to ventilate their feelings, the Top Three member who chaired the emergency meeting asked, without delay, for any objections to the resident staying. (Asking for objections is part of the "ritual"). Before anybody could respond the chairperson proclaimed that permission to stay was "granted". Staff challenged this foreclosing of the issue by pointing out the seriousness of Diana's behaviour and the inevitable emotional impact this must have had on other community members. This intervention was followed by a few desultory comments, conveyed without passion. In spite of repeated staff promptings, permission to stay on the Unit was granted in the absence of any real discussion.

The absence of a lively response from residents may have resulted from shock at the news of the dangerous behaviour and it might have been inappropriate for staff to attempt to introduce a discussion of the matter given the recency of the event. Interestingly, however, at the voting which followed the twenty-four assessment period there also was a similar reluctance on the part of the community to discuss the matter or confront Diana with the reality of the emotional impact of her behaviour on the community. Residents thus responded in a mechanical way, enforcing the rules, by which community members agree to live, without any real sense of relatedness to Diana. The community's authority was executed but in an unthinking and unfeeling manner as if the matter were a mere bureaucratic necessity. (Incidentally, this apathetic response mirrored the situation which obtained between Diana and her mother whom she had always felt powerless to influence).

* Eric had confided to another resident, during his first week on the Unit, that he had taken illicit drugs on the day of admission, both prior to and after arriving.

Leniency and tolerance are hallmarks of the community in consideration of "new residents". Nevertheless the "hard" nature of the drugs taken alarmed other members of the community and especially those with drug misuse histories who felt, in addition, envious of the fact that Eric had succumbed to temptation with which they were continuing to struggle. Permission to stay on the Unit, so that all parties concerned could reflect on the event, was quickly granted. On the day of the re-admission vote, there was little expression of the anxieties which Eric must have had in relation to being admitted and the chairperson (another male with a history of drug misuse) effectively stifled discussion by repeatedly asking if members "knew enough to vote", so that any debate quickly petered out. Staff's protestations, which were muted in view of the "newness" of the resident, were ineffective and failed to produce a more satisfactory airing of the issues. The leniency exercised by the community was not appreciated by Eric (as events were to indicate) and there was a further episode of drug misuse which on challenge from the community drew from him a hostile and defensive response. On this occasion extreme exasperation, with little sense of sympathy, was conveyed to Eric. He then took his own discharge the following day.

One of the issues here concerns the often fine dividing line between tolerance and neglect and represents an example of the community making a decision (via voting) without allowing itself to go through the attendant emotional impact which a thorough appraisal of the event would necessarily entail.

In the next clinical example, the community cuts short discussion and attempts to invoke a new rule. Thus the empowering of the residents' sub-system in influencing the community's structure, which is a core ingredient of therapeutic community ideology, is used without a genuine therapeutic aim.

*Clinical Example*

- In the group meeting during which residents' elections to the community's posts take place, there was a reluctance to fill a number of the more onerous and responsible posts. This reflected a number of factors: a recent influx of especially demanding "new residents"; consequent exhaustion on the part of more senior residents; and a general feeling of disempowerment of the residents' sub-system resulting from a recently discharged resident who had become psychotic. (Staff had assumed full responsibility for the transfer of this resident to a more traditional psychiatric hospital and also for the managing of the difficult behaviour which carried on after she had been "voted out" of the community but while she still remained on the premises).

   One unfilled post was that of the Social Work Liaison Officer SWLO. The incumbent accompanies residents who feel in need of support when keeping hospital or other appointments outside the Unit. The usual practice is that this post can be occupied by a resident of either sex. However, there are in fact two posts, the SWLO and an assistant SWLO, and if the incumbent of one is male then the other is female. In this instance the postholder should have been a woman. However, no women put forward their names and none accepted nominations by other resident members to be put forward. A male resident, who was keen to occupy the post, volunteered. A staff member pointed out this was contrary to the usual practice. Another male resident, (with a history of convictions and imprisonment for violence) aggressively insisted that the rule should be changed, arguing his case loudly. After a pause, most of the residents watched and listened apprehensively while the staff member stood his ground, agreeing that rules were indeed negotiated between staff and residents but only in the context of a community meeting. Most of the resident members rallied behind the staff member in agreeing that the "structure needed to be kept to". In the event, no appointment was made during the meeting (an unusual occurrence) and the post therefore remained temporarily vacant.

The above examples serve to stress the need for therapeutic community staff to remain alert, firstly, to the potential of the therapeutic culture being lost through a devitalisation of its structure and, secondly, to the various ways in which this might happen. Clearly, interventions of various sorts by staff (or resident members) can be delivered in the above situations drawing the attention of the community to the phenomenon. However, staff are inevitably also caught up in the same processes as residents. Therefore, identifying what is going on is not always so straightforward. Indeed, often parallel defensive manoeuvres take place in the staff group at the same time as they happen in the community at large, as if the prevailing dynamic issues, at any given time, are in both staff and resident subsystems (see Zinkin, 1987).

In a paper entitled "Knowledge, learning and freedom from thought", Main described the way in which an idea can pass from one person to another and "change its mental residence, moving from the thinking areas of the ego of one generation into the fixed morality areas, the ego ideal and the super-ego of the next" (Main, 1967). Frequently, Henderson staff attempt to remember rather than think in the face of problematic clinical situations. This avoids the emotional work entailed in achieving a work group level of functioning (Bion, 1963). Instead, staff search for existing "knowledge" or for an earlier precedent (much akin to some practices of law in wider society). The following clinical examples may help to illustrate the point.

*Clinical Examples*
- Recently a resident painted a picture (in washable paint) on the wall of his room.  It should be noted that there is conspicuous art work, sanctioned and produced by the community, which decorates a variety of locations and includes a mural. As well, there is a weekly art therapy group and also an art "work group" and open access to the art room and its materials at any time of day or night.  The matter was brought to the community by Top Three questioning whether the behaviour constituted damage to property, which would carry with it automatic discharge, although with the possibility of reinstatement subject to permission from the community.

  The community, staff and residents, became polarised on the issue. The meaning of the act for the individual resident could not be addressed in spite of an attempt by some staff to introduce this aspect into the discussion. In the staff's independent review of the community meeting, debate  continued with staff disagreeing with one another over whether the painting of the picture had been a creative or defiling act. The staff subsystem, like the residents' sub-system,  was preoccupied solely with the issue of whether a rule had been broken. What was lacking, at least for a time, was a capacity for either subsystem, together or separately, to "think" about the situation and reflect on the meaning of the action for the particular resident in the context of the community at that point in his therapy. In the absence of a "culture of enquiry" there was recourse to mindless structure the rules.

- In another community meeting there was an issue of whether "theft" carried out by a resident during therapy occasioned automatic discharge (with its attendant procedure as in above) or a similar assessment period followed by a discharge vote. Within the staff sub-system the debate continued afterwards in staff's separate review meeting. What was in evidence were attempts by individual staff members to recall precedents. This was carried on in a combative and competitive manner, rather than in a spirit of collaborative re-appraisal of what might be the logical or sensible response. Once more it was as if the capacity to think, "culture of enquiry", had been lost. (Of course, there is also a positive side to the staff sub-system's struggling in parallel with the same issues as the residents' and also within its own group context. In fact, it is such debates, at times fierce, which, paradoxically, enable the structure to remain alive and therapeutic communities may come to grief when such staff debate is habitually absent (Janzing, 1991).

- The staff dining facility was removed in an external re-organisation of premises beyond the control of the staff sub-system. Staff attempts to make alternative arrangements met with no success. There was an apparent consensus that eating together as staff had provided an informal interaction which was now sadly absent. In spite of the topic being repeatedly aired, and potentially viable solutions discussed, nothing happened. Details of none of the proposed schemes could be "thought through". It was as if the staff's capacity to think (as well as to influence external events) had been lost.

The therapeutic culture, whether handed down from more senior residents to newer residents, or from senior staff to new staff, is at risk of being de-vitalised by the unrecognised action of the types of processes just described. Paradoxically, newer residents and newer staff often resuscitate the culture by questioning the "established" version of the way things are done or not done (as in the case of lunching arrangements for staff). The initial, sometimes hostile, rebuttal which usually follows from more senior residents and staff, is at times followed by some genuine reflection on their part (depressive position functioning) and a mature discussion and this can facilitate a return to lost values.

## CONCLUSIONS

Main (1946, 1967, 1983) established some fundamental ideas and principles, the essence of which is still fresh and pertinent in today's therapeutic community, if Henderson Hospital's experience is representative. Other writers, too numerous to mention, have addressed, directly or indirectly, the cultural theme. In respect of Henderson Hospital, Jones (1952), Rapoport (1960) and, of course, Whiteley (1986) have all described important cultural aspects as well as defining its structure. In virtually all descriptive accounts of therapeutic communities in action an important cultural dimension is imparted, which is inevitable given the inter-relationship of the two concepts structure and culture. Nevertheless, the phrase "culture of enquiry", with the implication of thinking, reflecting and questioning, is especially relevant to a consideration of the treatment of individuals exhibiting borderline personality organisation (Kernberg, 1976) and hence for Henderson Hospital.

Masterson (1972), writing about therapy for such patients, stresses that the goal is their becoming "thinkers and feelers". Within therapeutic communities, a "culture of enquiry" may serve this goal through reinstating emotional conflict previously avoided. Such reinstatement involves the coming together of opposites (Jung, 1963) from which can evolve transforming solutions which are truly creative for the individual concerned (Storr, 1972). The important point, therefore, is  the extent to which contradictory elements (logical and illogical;  thought and feeling;  head and heart)  can exist together and work in concert. Thus the goal of treatment, "thinkers and feelers", has the emphasis on the "and". Without therapy it is as if residents can either "think" or "feel". There is thinking which is often devoid of feelings. There are feelings which cannot be contained or expressed verbally and, in effect, spill over into behaviour. The goal of treatment, therefore, is to facilitate a harnessing of feeling and thinking and to enable  the development of a capacity to maintain such a style.

A "culture of enquiry" does not imply, therefore, total intellectual detachment. This would not be a desirable or relevant goal, even though some degree of detachment from the grip of powerful destructive or maladaptive urges is clearly desirable both for the individual and for wider society, at least in most social situations. What is implied is a capacity to think with feeling (i.e. "thinker and feeler"), to be able to appraise both intellectually and emotionally. For this to happen the individual community member must experience a sense of being able to influence other community members, to affect them emotionally. Beyond this, the community needs to be able to deal with, both at the level of the individual and of the whole community, contradictory feelings and thoughts towards any members who overstep the limits imposed by virtue of the community's "structure", which necessarily exists to proscribe certain behaviours and permit others (Glen, 1975).

Much activity within organisations is designed (often not in a deliberately thought out way, but as a result of unconscious factors) to avoid emotional conflict (Jacques, 1955; Menzies, 1970). Behaviour, for instance, the use of formal job titles or uniforms for staff and Christian names for "patients", is of a gross kind and obvious, at least once its significance has been pointed out. This "macroscopic" analytic approach to organisations is invaluable and any institution is likely to benefit from an evaluation and examination of its gross structures and functioning. However, the influence of Main's writing, referred to in this paper, is also to highlight, what might be termed, "microscopic" influences which serve a similarly defensive function and which tend to obstruct the stated aims of the organisation. Thus both "macroscopic" and "microscopic" perspectives are required if all the pitfalls are to be uncovered. Staff members, in particular, need to remain vigilant for "macroscopic" and "microscopic" evidence that the structure has lost its life, so extinguishing its therapeutic culture.

Short-term loss of a "culture of enquiry" may not be damaging so long as it recovers spontaneously or action is taken to remedy the situation once the true state of affairs has been recognised. Without an awareness of the destructive potential of even seemingly trivial and minute departures from such a culture, insidiously destructive processes can develop which threaten the long-term survival of a given community. The burden of responsibility for awareness falls to staff by virtue of their particular role and function in the community. This demands allegiance to the basic principles and ideologies of the therapeutic community albeit in a thinking way.

As Kennard (1989) described, a democratic tendency (Winnicott, 1950) is important if a therapeutic culture is to take root and flourish. This implies a relatively mature capacity to think and to endure emotional conflict without seeking premature or inappropriate resolution through action or retreat. Such a tendency is required if the staff sub-system is to counterbalance and overcome, more often than not, its own tendency to degenerate into basic assumption group functioning. This is required since only if the staff sub-system is able to do this, often enough and well enough, can it influence the community as a whole in a therapeutic direction. This is often difficult to achieve, particularly because the work setting entails functioning in a large community meeting and other group settings which can enhance or exaggerate tendencies toward more immature modes of thinking, emotional expression and behaviour. Re-reading and re-discussing some of Main's seminal contributions, referred to in this paper, may assist staff in their struggles to understand and help their clients.

## REFERENCES

AMERICAN PSYCHIATRIC ASSOCIATION, (1980) *Diagnostic and Statistical Manual of Mental Disorders* (3rd Edition.) (DSM-III). Washington: APA.

BION, W.R. (1961) *Experiences in groups.* London: Heinemann.

BION, W.R. (1963) *Elements of psychoanalysis.* London: Heinemann.

BLAU, P.M. & SCOTT, W. (1968) *Formal organisations.* San Francisco: Chandler.

COID, J.N. (1990) Psychopathic disorders. *Current Opinions in Psychiatry* 2, pp 750-756.

COPAS, J.B. & WHITELEY, J.S. (1976) Predicting success in the treatment of psychopaths. *British Journal of Psychiatry*, pp 129, 388-392.

DE MARE, P. (1985) Large group perspectives. *Group Analysis.* XVIII/2, pp 79-92.

DEROGATIS, L.R., LIPMAN, R.S. & COVI, L. (1973) SCL-90: an out-patient psychiatric rating scale - preliminary report. *Psychopharmacology Bulletin,* 9(1), pp 13-28.

DOLAN, B., MORTON, A. & WILSON, J. (1990) Selection of admissions to a therapeutic community using a group setting: Association with degree and type of psychological distress. *International. Journal of Social Psychiatry* 36(4), pp 265-271.

DOLAN, B., WILSON, J. & EVANS, C.D.H. (1992) Therapeutic community treatment for personality disordered adults: Changes in neurotic symptomatology on follow-up. *International Journal of Social Psychiatry* 38(4): pp 243-250.

DOLAN, B., POLLEY, K., ALLEN R. & NORTON, K. (1991) Addressing racism in psychiatry: is the therapeutic community model applicable? *International Journal of Social Psychiatry.* 37(2), pp 71-79.

DOLAN, B. EVANS, C.D.H. and NORTON, K.R.W. (1992) The Separation-Individuation Inventory: association with borderline phenomena. *Journal of Nervous* and *Mental Disease* 180(8) pp 529-533.

GLEN, F. (1975) *The social psychology of organisations.* London: Methuen and Co. Ltd.

GROVE, W.M. and TELLEGEN, A. (1991) Problems in the classification of personality disorders. *Journal of Personality Disorders.* 5(1), pp 31- 41.

HINSHELWOOD, R.D. & GRUNBERG, S. (1979) The large group syndrome. In: *Therapeutic Communities: Reflections and progress.* (Eds) Hinshelwood, R.D. and Manning, N. London: Routledge and Kegan Paul Ltd.

JACQUES, E. (1955) Social systems as a defence against persecutory and depressive anxiety. In: *New Directions in Psychoanalysis.* (Eds) Klein, M., Heimann, P. and Money-Kyrle, R. London: Tavistock Publications.

JANZIG, C. (1991) One Foot in Hell: on self-destructive staff dynamics. *International Journal of Therapeutic Communities,* 12,1, pp 5-12.

JONES, M. (1952) *Social psychiatry.* Tavistock Books: London.

JUNG, C.G. (1963) The conjunction. *Collected Works,* 14, pp 645-658.

KENNARD, D. (1979) Limiting factors: the setting, the staff, the patients. In: *Therapeutic Communities: Reflections and Progress.* Eds. Hinshelwood, R.D. and Manning, N. London: Rout- ledge and Kegan Paul.

KENNARD, D. (1989) The therapeutic impulse: what makes it grow? *International Journal of Therapeutic Communities,* 10,(3), pp 155-163.

KERNBERG, O. (1976) *Object relations theory and clinical psychoanalysis.* New York: Jason Aronson.

KLEIN, M. (1935) A contribution to the psychogenesis of manic- depressive states. *International Journal of Psycholanalysis,* 16, 1.

LAMBERT, K. (1981) *Analysis, repair and individuation.* London: Academic Press.

MAIN, T. (1946) The hospital as a therapeutic institution. *Bull. Menninger Clinic,* 10, pp 66-68.

MAIN, T. (1967) Knowledge, learning and freedom from thought. *Aust. N.Z. Journal of Psychiatry,* 1: pp 64-71.

MAIN, T. (1983) The concept of the therapeutic community: variations and vicissitudes. In: *The evolution of group analysis.* Ed. Pines, M. London: Routledge and Kegan Paul Ltd.

MANNING, N. (1980) Collective disturbance in institutions: A sociological view of crisis and collapse. *International Journal of Therapeutic Communities,* 1, pp 147-158.

MANNING, N. (1989) *The therapeutic community movement: charisma and routinization.* London: Routledge.

MANOR, O. (1979) *Social roles and behavioural change.* Ph.D. Thesis, University of London.

MASTERSON, J. (1972) *Treatment of the borderline adolescent: a developmental approach.* New York: Wiley.

MENZIES, I.E.P. (1970) *The functioning of social systems as a defence against anxiety.* Centre for applied social research. London: Tavistock Institute of Human Relations.

NORRIS, M. (1983) Changes in patients during treatment at Henderson Hospital therapeutic community during 1977-1981. *British Journal of Med. Psychol.*, 56, pp 135-143.

NORTON, K. (1990) The significance and importance of the therapeutic community working practice. *International Journal of Therapeutic Communities.* 11(2), pp 67-76.

NORTON, K.R.W. (1992) Treating personality disordered individuals: the Henderson Hospital model. *Criminal Behaviour and Mental Health,* 2: pp 180-191

O'BRIEN, M. (1976) *Psychopathic disorder.* PhD. Thesis. University of London.

PERERA, S.B. (1989)   Ritual integration of aggression in psychotherapy.   In:   *The Borderline Personality in analysis.* Eds. Schwartz-Salant, N. and Stein, M. Illinois: Chiron Publications.

RAPOPORT, R. (1960) *The Community as Doctor.* London: Tavistock.

STORR, A. (1972) *The dynamics of creation.* London: Martin Secker and Warburg Ltd.

USANDIVARAS, R. (1985) The therapeutic process as a ritual. *Group Analysis,* XVIII/I, pp 8-17.

WHITELEY, J.S. (1970) The response of psychopaths to a therapeutic community. *British Journal of Psychiatry,* 116, pp 517-529.

WHITELEY, J.S. (1980) The Henderson Hospital. *International Journal of Therapeutic Communities,* 1, pp 38-58.

WHITELEY, J.S. (1986) Sociotherapy and psychotherapy in the treatment of personality disorder. *Journal of the Royal Society of Medicine,* Vol. 79, December.

WILSON, J. (1985) Leaving home as a theme in a therapeutic community. *International Journal of Therapeutic Communities,* 6(2), pp 71-78.

WINER, J.A. and LEWIS, L. (1984)   Interpretative psychotherapy in the inpatient community meeting. *Psychiatry,* 47, pp 333-341.

WINNICOTT, D.W. (1950) Some thoughts on the meaning of the word "democracy". Republished in *Home is Where we Start From.* Harmondsworth: Pelican.

WORLD HEALTH ORGANISATION (1978) *Manual of the ninth revision of the International Classification of Diseases* (ICD-9) Geneva: WHO.

YALOM, I.D. (1975) *The theory and practice of group psychotherapy.* New York: Basic Books

ZINKIN, L. (1987) The hologram as a model of analytical psychology. *Journal of Analytical Psychol.* 32, (1), 1, pp 1-22.

ZINKIN, L. (1989) The grail and the group. *Journal of Analytical Psychol.* 34, (4), pp 371-386.

# Addressing Racism in Psychiatry:
## Is the Therapeutic Community Model Applicable?

Bridget Dolan, Kevin Polley, Ruth Allen & Kingsley Norton.

*International Journal of Social Psychiatry*
*1991, Vol. 37: pp 71-79*

Several reports have documented the failure of statutory psychiatric services in Britain to provide for the needs of clients from minority ethnic groups. Black clients are particularly under-represented in psychotherapy services, the reasons for which are complex and varied, but include the institutionalised racism which pervades British society. We argue that the Therapeutic Community model of treatment (or aspects of it deployed in other mental health situations) provides a potential for a less racist service. Using the Henderson Hospital therapeutic community as a case in point, we argue that the therapeutic community is an approach which can meet the needs of black peoples. However, it is acknowledged that despite the *ideological* suitability of the therapeutic community model for black clients, in *practice* the Henderson Hospital is not fulfilling its role in providing therapy to this group. We discuss possible explanations and suggest the practical changes necessary, so that Henderson Hospital can meet the needs of clients in a multi-cultural Britain.

## INTRODUCTION

Racism can be described as "the specific belief that cultural differences between ethnic groups are biological in origin and that groups should be ranked in worth" (Littlewood and Lipsedge 1989). Richardson and Lambert

(1985) have identified three associated aspects of racism: as ideology; as practice and as a social structure (institutionalised racism).   Racism may operate through overt beliefs and actions of the individual (active racism) or through less conscious attitudes in society as a whole,   for example not offering housing,   education or care to ethnic groups (aversive racism). Littlewood and Lipsedge (1989) point out how anyone in a society who benefits by racism is,   in some measure,   a racist.   The racist is the normal individual in a racist society.

The effects of racism in British psychiatry are obvious,   although the racism itself is often more aversive than active.   Yet the racism in psychiatry is frequently played down.   Fernando (1988) notes the importance of the public face of psychiatry and how to point out racism in psychiatry will shake the position of psychiatry and threaten it.   This is clearly illustrated in a recent study which showed that British psychiatrists perceive a greater risk of violence from a black patient than a white,   and would more often suggest that police involvement is appropriate when a patient is black.   The authors concluded that this finding was not 'racism' and the concept should be avoided.   Despite some objections (*inter alia* Dolan and Evans, 1990)   this proposal was carried in a major British psychiatry journal (Lewis, Croft-Jeffreys and David,   1990).

It is apparent that black people are offered and receive a far inferior service to that of the indigenous British population in all aspects of housing, employment social and health care,   (Brown,   1984;   Francis,   David, Johnson and Sashidharan,   1989).   Paradoxically,   however,   there is an overrepresentation of black,   mainly Afro-Caribbean,   peoples in psychiatric facilities (London,   1986; Cochrane,   1977; Carpenter and Brockington,   1980; Harrison *et al.*,   1988).

It has been consistently shown that black people are far more likely than white to be labelled with diagnoses related to psychotic illnesses (Littlewood and Lipsedge,   1981; Littlewood,   1988).   Diagnostic categorisation in psychiatry is of importance,   among other reasons,   for it is the major indicator of the 'appropriate' treatment and hence is of relevance in the provision of appropriate services.   Not only are black people more often diagnosed psychotic but,   as a consequence of this,   black people are more likely to receive enforced treatment,   to be prescribed psychotropic medication and to be kept in hospital longer (Dunn and Fahy,   1990) often in seclusion or on locked wards (McGovern and Cope, 1987). This form of treatment is often to the exclusion of any psychotherapy or social interventions. The over-representation of black clients under the various sections of the Mental Health Act is another area of serious concern which requires further understanding (Dunn and Fahy, 1987, 1990). Enforced treatment approaches, involving loss of personal liberty, place the recipient in a state of subjugation and powerlessness. In this way the institution of the NHS is adding to the experience of subjugation and alienation received by black people from other aspects of British society. Psychological tests, which are used to 'assess' and 'understand' the client, have usually been developed using the White Anglo-Saxon male as the "normal group" and discriminate against minority groups both in terms of test construction and the inferences drawn from test results.

Racism in psychiatry is not only directed towards the patients. The bias against people of minority groups in employment and promotion within various professions of health service has been shown (Fernando, 1988). In the selection of medical students discrimination against non-white and female applicants is clear (Collier and Burke, 1986).

The NHS like all social institutions is culture bound, and as such favours the needs of the dominant groups and fails to provide equitable services for other groups (Chau, 1990). Not surprisingly the experiences of black people within NHS psychiatry have often been negative and have led to a distrust of mainstream psychiatry. Thus representatives of black communities have requested a different approach to service provision without the prejudice which currently operates (Francis *et al.*, 1989; Acharyya, Moorhouse, Kareem and Littlewood, 1989). Black mental health groups have developed and called for an approach to therapy which avoids the use of 'chemical straitjackets'. However, it is also within NHS psychotherapy, that black clients are under-represented (Campling, 1989). The reasons accounting for this may be complex but this is an unacceptable state of affairs and, in part, another example of institutionalised racism. Action, as well as understanding, is required. One response to this situation has been the expeditious growth of organisations within black communities which provide counselling and support for black people by black people (Acharyya *et al.*, 1989; Francis *et al.*, 1989). This must be seen in part to be because of the failure of aspects of statutory services to meet black clients' needs.   However, services provided by black professionals for black clients may not be intrinsically superior.   Thus attentive responses are required in terms of services which actively orientate themselves to the needs of minority clients and relative efficiencies evaluated (Nafsiyat, 1988).

This paper documents the argument that the Therapeutic Community model of treatment (and possibly aspects of it deployed in other mental health situations) can,  with modification based upon awareness of racist issues,  offer a potential for a less racist service delivery.  Of particular importance in the context of this argument is the therapeutic community model's ideological departure from the medical model which pervades mainstream psychiatry and which is often found also in traditional psychotherapy.  Using the Henderson Hospital therapeutic community as a case in point,  it is argued that the therapeutic community is an approach to mental health care which can meet the needs of black peoples.   It is acknowledged,   however,   that despite the *ideological* suitability of the therapeutic community model for black clients,  in practice the therapeutic community is not fulfilling its role in providing therapy to this group. Possible reasons for this and what practical changes need to be made in a unit such as Henderson Hospital,  so that it is able to meet the needs of black clients,  are discussed below.

**THE THERAPEUTIC COMMUNITY MODEL**

The term Therapeutic Community was coined in the 1940's (Main, 1946).  It denotes some of the changes which have occurred in psychiatric hospitals emphasising a move away from an authoritarian system toward a collaborative style of staff behaviour and a more active participation of patients in their own treatment.  This model and approach to treatment has since spread into fields of community based residential care,  day hospitals, concept houses etc.  A central idea is the combination of interventions relating to the psychological world and to the social world of the community's members (Blake and Millard, 1979).

The Therapeutic Community model was chiefly pioneered by Maxwell Jones and others in Belmont Hospital Industrial Rehabilitation Unit later renamed as Henderson Hospital when it became autonomous thirty years ago (Jones, 1952;  1982).  Henderson Hospital is an NHS funded therapeutic community which offers therapy mainly for personality disordered adults (Whiteley,   1980).   There are today several types of institutions which follow a therapeutic community approach,  so that a single 'representative' therapeutic community is difficult to describe (Bloor *et al.*, 1988).  However in Britain the Maxwell Jones-type model is associated with 'therapeutic community proper' and exemplified by Henderson (Clark,    1965). Sociological study of Henderson revealed that four major ideological themes,   reflecting variations away from traditional hospital ideology, pervaded the community structure and these were termed Communalism, Permissiveness,   Democratisation and Reality Confrontation (Rapoport, 1960).  In practice the emphasis is that the daily life of the Therapeutic Community must be "relevant to the needs and aspirations of the small society of the hospital and to the larger society in which it is set" (Main, 1946).  What is argued here is that a therapeutic community model should, despite being part of mainstream psychiatry and embedded as it is in a racist Britain,  be able to redress the racism in psychiatry at least to an extent.  For this to be so,  however,  requires that the therapeutic community is aware of the wider social system in which it finds itself and in relation to which it has to exist.  This cannot deny the reality that therapeutic communities grew from an ethnocentric white society.  Thus,  illustrating this it has only been recently that there has been much discussion of what racism and a racist society mean to therapy at Henderson,  and what action should be taken to better integrate Henderson into,  and to provide a service for,  a multi-cultural Britain.

As an NHS unit Henderson must maintain clear communication with other components of the NHS.  This relies,  to an extent,  upon a shared language,   of which psychiatric classification and jargon form part. Nonetheless,   medical models and stereotypes prevalent in mainstream psychiatry are not strongly taken up at Henderson.  Indeed,  attempts are made to avoid repeating the negative stereotypes of society.

The staff team comprises doctors,   nurses and other mental health professionals who are,  to some extent labelled with their profession,  paid salaries according to their professional level,   and answerable to their professional bodies etc.  However,  the lack of formal staff roles,  in respect to most therapeutic tasks,  the absence of uniforms,  the use of first names, and the appropriate sharing of responsibility within the entire community (staff and residents) minimise reinforcement of the medical model. Community members are called "residents", rather than patients. No psychotropic medicine is used in therapy nor can any resident be admitted to Henderson under a Probation Order with a condition of treatment, nor under any section of the Mental Health Act. The aim is to produce an atmosphere which avoids reinforcing the power relationship intrinsic to therapist and patient. Therapy at Henderson takes place in formal group settings (there is no individual therapy) and informally via the social milieu. The aspiration is that the major 'doctor' in the community is the community itself.

Formal psychiatric diagnosis beyond 'personality disorder' is rarely referred to within Henderson (and then usually only among staff). This avoids some reinforcing of stereotypic labels which might cause still more stigma. 'Symptoms' are not the focus of therapy, instead the community concentrates upon the meaning of individuals' feelings or actions, in the context of their relationships with others (residents and staff). This avoidance of psychiatric labels and focus on symptomatology may be of particular importance for the black client given the problems in applying Western diagnostic 'universals' to describe the experiences and emotions of people from non-western cultures (Kirmayer, 1989). The referral procedure at Henderson allows for individuals to refer themselves for treatment or for referral to come from family members, counsellors or voluntary organisations. Thus a psychiatric diagnosis (label) is not needed to ensure referral. However, 55% of our referrals are from psychiatrists, and the vast majority of our residents have previously had psychiatric treatment. Henderson's close contact with mainstream psychiatry, location within the NHS and reliance upon psychotherapeutic methods means that it will still evoke many negative associations for black potential residents.

The issue of differential service usage is of concern in all aspects of psychiatry and psychotherapy (Rwegellera, 1980; Campling, 1989) not only therapeutic community work. The ability to self refer may not be enough to encourage black people to learn about or use what remains predominantly a white service. Additionally, the use of group interaction and discussion may be a particularly alienating style for some black peoples. Since the therapeutic community is predominantly a verbal culture, it is necessary for residents to express feelings in English. This automatically excludes from therapy those who do not speak English and may be problematic for some people for whom English is not a first language. The daily programme, based predominantly upon a Monday to Friday 9-5 working week, may be alien to people of some cultures, and certainly does not readily allow time within it for observance of the religious practices of Judaism or Islam.

If the key issues in racism are of marginality and oppression, the life experience of most of Henderson's non-black clients is one also characterised by increasing marginality and isolation. Many clients will have been labelled by society as "mentally ill", "unemployable", "delinquent", "untreatable" etc. Such labelling will have been used both to withhold services and facilities, and in effect to control and oppress the individual. In fact, individuals such as those admitted to Henderson have been stereotyped as "the patients psychiatrists dislike" (Lewis and Appleby, 1988). Such statements as this represent part of a process which is similar to the process of marginalisation and oppression which is experienced by black peoples in white society and reproduced in mainstream psychiatry. White and black residents sharing this common experience is an important aspect of Henderson therapy. Living and learning in the social system of the therapeutic community allows a group identity to form which lessens feelings of vulnerability and isolation of the individual.

Democratisation is a major feature of Henderson culture. Residents have a large responsibility for the day to day running of the unit, they play a major role in deciding who is admitted and the timing of discharge, in defining rules and in how rules are interpreted, applied and carried out. Most decisions are made on a consensus basis or on a one person one vote principle. This democratisation and shared decision making provides a culture in which every individual has at least the opportunity to feel equally important. The result can be an experience of empowerment which may be unfamiliar to those who have experienced prejudice and oppression because of any personal characteristic, be this race, culture, gender, sexuality or disability. Research at Henderson has demonstrated the enhancement of self-esteem as a result of the treatment (Norris, 1983).

It cannot be claimed that racist attitudes do not exist within Henderson Hospital community members. Racism is ubiquitous in our society even if unconsciously expressed (Nafsiyat, 1988, note that two-thirds of their patients in therapy had experienced racism in the previous three months). Racist comments and 'jokes' are sometimes made at Henderson and occasionally more overtly racist feelings are declared. However, the 'reality confrontation' ideology of Henderson enables people's prejudices to be confronted in the here and now at any time. Therefore an expression of racism in the therapeutic community of Henderson Hospital may allow an individual to understand his or her own part in it, either as the perpetrator or recipient. Power relations and racism can be recognised and faced as live issues in therapy if the community contains both black and white residents a situation not often achieved in other treatment settings or institutions. Re-living any experience can be worked with therapeutically, even if this process is a difficult one. A client can use his or her time in the community to work through former experiences (e.g. in psychodrama) and experiment with new strategies for coping with and learning from it. The therapeutic space may allow staff and residents to get in touch with their own potential for racism and to develop counter-strategies for dealing with or unlearning prejudice.

Communalism an integral part of the therapeutic community model can enable people to learn to accept each other as individuals regardless of their different backgrounds. In some cases residents may be exposed to people of a social or cultural background which they have not previously encountered or understood. This provides some of the raw materials from which a greater tolerance and respect for individual differences may be built.

However, a claim that the aspects mentioned above enable the therapeutic community to meet the needs of black clients is a presumptive judgement that these needs are actually known. In a predominantly white community understanding the needs of black people in Britain is difficult. It would seem to be important not to assume knowledge of these needs, nor to guess that the needs of each black person will be the same. The family ties, interpersonal and authority relationships, with which so many Henderson residents wrestle in therapy, may have different meanings for black peoples living within a different social structure. There will be meanings in relationships and behaviours of which white staff and residents are largely ignorant and these cannot then inform appropriate therapeutic judgements and strategies. The gender mixing of the community may have different implications for women and men of differing cultural backgrounds.

In conclusion, the therapeutic community model can, in theory, offer a model of treatment which may be more appropriate for and acceptable to some people from black communities. Nonetheless, the fact that less than 10% of current Henderson residents are black suggests that at the present time the therapeutic community model of itself, does not translate, in practice, into an adequate service to black peoples. It is obvious then that ideological appropriateness is not enough. Henderson, as an example of the therapeutic community proper, itself requires some changes. It has already undergone one change, perhaps of similar magnitude, with the move to admit women to a totally male unit in the 1960's. Mixing of the genders was a long term task, which was only possible alongside fundamental changes in outlook, staff team composition, treatment approach and to some extent in ideology. Over two decades later Collis noted that sexist ideologies still disempowered women at Henderson (Collis 1985). In passing it should be noted that female residents outnumbered male for the first time in 1989.

Increasing the numbers of black residents and staff to provide an informal, supportive, and understanding environment is perhaps the most necessary change. However, a broad multi-ethnic mix representative of different cultural groups would be impossible to achieve and maintain. Few black people are referred for treatment at Henderson approximately 1 in 50 referrals. Henderson is not unusual in this for it is well established that there is an extremely low rate of referral of black people for psychotherapy (Campling, 1989) and for other specialist psychiatric services (e.g. Lacey and Dolan, 1988). In contrast almost one quarter of referrals to Nafsiyat, a non-statutory sector intercultural therapy centre, are self-referred. It is tempting to place the responsibility for low referral rates solely on the referrers, but until existing services are made appropriate and acceptable to black peoples it cannot be expected that they will be taken up. Although Henderson has adopted a policy of liaising with black organisations, its ability to do this and to increase referral of black clients has been so far unsatisfactory. Henderson is only at the starting point of change. Taking the inherent risks of change seem both worthwhile and necessary if Henderson is to fulfil its obligations to offer a service for all people in a multi-ethnic Britain. Not only do the causes of the low referral rate need to be understood but action will also be taken to secure referrals.

## CONCLUSIONS

In summary, in this paper we have examined how one model of mental health care delivery, the therapeutic community, can begin to address the institutionalised racism in British psychiatry at least for a sub-group of those in psychiatric need. We do not suggest that the therapeutic community model is the only applicable model. However, we have concentrated upon how, in our unit, ideologically and in practice the therapeutic community approach has some potential advantages over a more traditional medical model for black clients. Some individual facets of therapeutic community philosophy and practice may be generalisable to other institutions and models.

We contend that there may be aspects of the more traditional medical model approach which might be inadvertently reinforcing racism via an effect extended through the 'power' imbalance intrinsic of patient-doctor relationship. We recommend that others could examine their own ideology and working practices, as we have begun to do, with the aim of identifying any such influences which may impact negatively on the treatment of their black clients. Our own experience suggests that a thoughtful but passive approach to problems of inappropriately low referral or service take up of black clients should be abandoned. We would advocate a policy for action which includes, for example, liaison with non-statutory black treatment groups to generate appropriate referrals; positive discrimination in favour of black clients (when the structure of the service provides this) and paying attention to the composition of the staff team with respect to ethnic mix.

## REFERENCES

ACHARYYA, S., MOORHOUSE, S., KAREEM, J., LITTLEWOOD, R. (1989) Nafsiyat: A psychotherapy centre for ethnic minorities *Psychiatric Bulletin* 13, *pp* 358-360.

BLAKER, MILLARD, D. (1979*) The Therapeutic Community in day care: A guide to planning.* London, ATC.

BLOOR, M., McKENAGY, N., FONKERT D. (1988) *One foot in Eden: A sociological study of the range of Therapeutic Community practice* Routledge, London.

BROWN, C. (1984) *Black and White in Britain: The third PSI survey.* London, Heinemann.

CAMPLING, P. (1989) Black people and psychotherapy *Psychiatric Bulletin 13,* pp 550-551

CARPENTER, L. AND BROCKINGTON, I. F. (1980) A study of mental illness in Asians, West Indians and Africans living in Manchester. *British Journal of Psychiatry* 137, pp 201-205

CHAU, K. L. (1990) Social work with groups in a multicultural con text. *Groupwork* 3(1) pp 8-21.

CLARK, D. H. (1965) The Therapeutic Community Concept: Present and Future. *British Journal of Psychiatry* 111; pp 947-954.

COCHRANE, R. (1977) Mental illness in immigrants to England and Wales: An analysis of mental hospital admissions, 1971. *Social Psychiatry* 12, pp 25-35.

COLLIER, J. , BURKE, A (1986) Racial and sexual discrimination in the selection of students for London medical schools *Medical Education* 20, pp 86-90.

COLLIS, M. (1985) Women's groups in the therapeutic community *International Journal of Therapeutic Communities* 8(3), pp 175-184

DEAN, G. , WALSH, D. , DOWNING, H. AND SHELLEY, E. (1981). First admissions of native born and immigrants to psychiatric hospitals in South East England 1976. *British Journal of Psychiatry* 139, pp 506-512.

DOLAN, B. , EVANS, C. (1990) The Bowlderisation of Psychiatry *British Journal of Psychiatry* 157, pp 936-937.

DUNN, J. , FAHY, T. (1987) Section 136 and the police. *Psychiatric Bulletin* 11, pp 224-225.

DUNN, J., FAHY, T. (1990) Police admissions to psychiatric hospital: Demographic and clinical differences between ethnic groups *British Journal of Psychiatry* 156, pp 373-378.

FERNANDO, S. (1988) *Race and Culture in Psychiatry.* London, Croom Helm.

FRANCIS, E., DAVID, J., SASHIDHARAN, S. P. (1989) Black people and psychiatry in the UK. *Psychiatric Bulletin* 13, pp 482-485.

HARRISON, G., OWENS, D., HOLTON, A., NEILSON, D., BOOT, D. (1988) A prospective study of severe mental disorder in Afro Caribbean patients *Psychological Medicine* 18, pp 643-657.

JONES, M. (1952) *Social Psychiatry.* Tavistock, London.

JONES, M. (1982) *The Process of Change.* Routledge & Kegan Paul, London.

KIRMAYER, L. J. (1989) Cultural variations in response to psychiatric disorders and emotional distress. *Social Science & Medicine* 29(3), pp 327-339.

LACEY, J. H., DOLAN, B. M. (1988) Bulimia in British blacks and Asians: A catchment area study *British Journal of Psychiatry* 152, pp 73-77.

LEWIS, G., APPLEBY, D. (1988) Personality disorders: The patients psychiatrists dislike. *British Journal of Psychiatry* 153, pp 44-49.

LEWIS, G., CROFT JEFFREYS, C., DAVID, A. (1990) Are British psychiatrists racist ? *British Journal of Psychiatry* 157, pp 410-415.

LITTLEWOOD, R. AND LIPSEDGE, M. (1981) Psychiatric illness amongst British Afro-Caribbeans *British Medical Journal* 296, pp 950 951.

LITTLEWOOD, R., LIPSEDGE, M. (1989) *Aliens and Alienists* 2nd edition, London, Unwin Hyman.

LONDON, M. (1986) Mental illness amongst immigrant minorities in the United Kingdom. *British Journal of Psychiatry* 149, pp 265-273.

MAIN, T. (1946) The hospital as a therapeutic institution. *Bulletin of Menninger Clinic* 10, pp 66.

McGOVERN, D., COPE, R. (1987) The compulsory detention of males of different ethnic groups with special reference to offender patients. *British Journal of Psychiatry* 150, pp 505-512.

NAFSIYAT (1988) *Nafsiyat Intercultural Therapy Centre: The first five years: A report.* Unpublished Document, Nafsiyat, London.

NORRIS, M. (1983) Changes in patients during admission to Henderson Hospital therapeutic community during 1977-1981. *British Journal of Medical Psychology* 56: pp 135-143.

RACK, P. (1982) Migration and mental illness: A review of recent research in Britain *Transcultural Psychiatry Research Review* 19; pp 151-172.

RAPOPORT, R. N (1960) *Community as Doctor.* Tavistock, London.

RICHARDSON, J. , LAMBERT, J. (1985) *The sociology of Race* Lancs, Causeway Press.

RWEGELLERA, G. G. C. (1980) Differential use of psychiatric services by West Indians, West Africans and English in London *British Journal of Psychiatry* 137, pp 428-432.

VARMA, V. K. (1988) Culture, personality and psychotherapy *International Journal of Social Psychiatry* 34(2); pp 142-149.

**ACKNOWLEDGEMENTS***This paper was presented in the form of a live debate at - The Association of Therapeutic Communities Conference (June, 1990) "Therapeutic Communities, Race and Culture".  We are grateful to the entire staff  team at Henderson Hospital for their contributions to this paper.*

# Acting Out and the Institutional Response

Kingsley Norton & Bridget Dolan

*The Journal of Forensic Psychiatry*
*1995, Vol. 6: pp 317-332*

The responses of institutions to 'acting out' in personality disordered individuals may perpetuate such behaviour. Inadvertently, such responses remove the potential for these individuals to learn from experience and to mature psychologically, to individualise. This is because institutions, first and foremost, serve the needs of society. In performing this wider function, they often do not meet, sufficiently, the therapeutic needs of the individual. The result is a stalemate in which both the individual who acts out and the institution continue to suffer.

An awareness of the interaction between the individual and the 'institution', and particularly an awareness of the often complementary style of their interaction, victim victimiser, may empower professionals working in institutions to break the therapeutic stalemate. However, to achieve this requires changes in attitudes and behaviour on the part of staff and some restructuring of the internal organisation of their institutions so as to influence both staff-staff and staff-patient relationships. We discuss how some principles of Henderson Hospital's democratic therapeutic community model, which helps to avoid some of the clinical pitfalls which otherwise can lead to therapeutic stalemate, can be translated to institutions which must of necessity operate at different levels of security and how they may be applied in non-specialist settings.

Ms. Jones is 'twenty and a psychiatric in-patient with a diagnosis of antisocial personality disorder. At 2 a.m. she injures herself with a 'Stanley' knife blade having threatened to do so the previous day after hearing distressing family news from home. She claims she was trying to cut off her breasts.   The nurse on duty inspects the wounds to Ms. Jones' breasts, applies dressings and contacts medical staff to discuss further management. Suturing is not indicated and no further medical attention is required.   What follows is a range of potential responses, for example, sedation, 'specialing', or seclusion, the actual response depending upon the nature of the institution, hospital and ward policies; the individual characteristics of the staff involved in managing the incident and the nature and quality of their relationship with the patient.

A characteristic feature of many personality disordered individuals is their impulsive and destructive behaviour, which often leads to a presentation to professionals in the midst of a crisis, emotional and/ or physical.   Such behaviour inevitably affects the healthcare staff involved in managing such a crisis, as in the above clinical vignette, and it often elicits a behavioural response from them in the form of a treatment intervention such as specialing, seclusion or sedation.   In many instances clinical management focuses solely on the physical containment, or removal, of those behaviours. Creating and maintaining a treatment alliance with severely personality disordered patients is difficult, even though the patient's behavioural component is often clearly recognised by staff to be but a surface marker of a deeper level of emotional problems in the individual, which are thereby masked.   Treatment of such patients is usually an arduous business with success, in non-specialist settings, elusive.   Unfortunately, this whole area, which is of major clinical concern, is poorly researched, as has been recently demonstrated by the UK Governmental Review of Services for Mentally Disordered Offenders (Reed, 1994; Dolan and Coid, 1993).

In the UK, the importance of providing adequate treatment and care for personality disordered patients is indicated by statements within the Prison Service Corporate Plan for 1993-6, which specify the core responsibility of the prison service for transferring mentally disordered offenders to care and treatment in the NHS and "where transfer is not possible to develop a strategy of management and treatment within the prison system of those prisoners suffering from personality disorders" (H.M. Prison Service, 1993 p.23). Even when in-patient services are provided for those with impulsive and self-destructive behaviour their adequacy is questioned by the high levels of violence inside hospital institutions (Aquilina, 1991; Powell, Caan and Crowe, 1994). A comprehensive report of the Health and Safety Commission expressed deep concern over the levels of violence to health service staff (HSC, 1987) and a recent survey (Thomas *et al.*, 1995) found that 39 per cent of psychiatric in-patients had been struck by another patient at least once during their hospital admission. Although many such violent incidents involve psychotic patients and those with mental impairment or learning disability, those with personality disorder also contribute appreciably to the total number of incidents (Powell *et al.*, 1994).

Much impulsive and destructive behaviour in personality disordered patients is described as "acting out" a term which is widely used but often imprecisely defined. Essentially, acting out involves an enactment of unconscious emotional conflict, which is usually impulsive, experienced with a sense of immediacy and often performed as a "scenario of great fidelity" (Laplanche and Pontalis, 1983), meaning that the activity is, as if, quite precisely scripted and rehearsed, albeit unconsciously so. In this way, conscious remembering of emotional conflict does not occur, but is replaced instead by action (Crockett, 1966). Acting out implies a narrowing of the patient's potential behavioural repertoire in response to a situation (inner or outer world) which would otherwise generate or re-awaken an experience of emotional conflict. (A typical example is the personality disordered in-patient who self-mutilates rather than seeking support and speaking about distress in the face of dispute or disappointment). It is the relative fixity of such responses which contributes importantly to the therapeutic stalemate often resulting from the interaction of the acting-out individual and a given institution since the tenacity with which such behaviour is held by the patient serves to confound and frustrate staff, with a resultant impairment of the professional relationship.

The nature and extent of the damage and violence accompanying much acting out often elicits a strong emotional reaction from those around the acting out patient, including relevant staff members, even from those not immediately involved. The type and intensity of the personal emotional component of such reactions obviously varies from staff to staff, however, the staff's professional role often makes the direct expression of their emotions questionable and professionalism, if not also the policy of the ward or hospital, may prohibit such expression.  The result may be staff struggling to keep silent or else to find words to cloak difficult negative emotions and to inhibit a behavioural response which, like much acting out behaviour, may also be aggressive. The way in which, and extent to which, staff are enabled to find a way of dealing with a potential conflict between their own personal and professional aspects will colour their, and hence the institutional, response to the acting out. The less well any mismatch between the staff's personal and professional components is handled the less therapeutic will be any response to a patient's acting out.  When the staff's personal response cannot be metabolised and translated into a professional level intervention, which still carries the conviction of the personal response but without undue aggression or outrage, then the possibility of an empathic connection with the patient is lost, and, without this the treatment alliance is difficult to sustain.  The result may be a response which is wooden and unnatural (perhaps rationalised as neutral or professional) or else partial, as if simply condoning or, alternatively, simply condemning.   As a consequence, what may be evoked in the patient is (1) more acting out, as if in an attempt to elicit from staff a genuine emotional response;   (2) withdrawal of serious emotional investment in treatment; or (3) withdrawal which is masked by a superficial appearance of compliance or co-operation with treatment.

Many psychiatric hospitals are, in effect, like acting out patients, in that they tend to display only a narrow repertoire of relatively inflexible responses, which serve the objectives of wider society.  Unwittingly, certain of these institutional responses to acting out behaviour (both those antecedent and consequent to the behaviour) can serve to escalate rather than ameliorate such behaviour, to the detriment of both the patient and the institution.  This paper examines aspects of the interaction between acting out patients and hospitals as they deploy their respective narrow behavioural repertoires, with the aim of identifying what maximises the likelihood that such a patient stops 'acting', becomes a 'thinker and feeler' (Masterson, 1972) and, in the process, becomes more fully himself or herself i.e. individualises.

## INTERACTIONS WITH THE HOSPITAL AS AN INSTITUTION

The conventional psychiatric institution, because of its largely custodial function, provides a limited repertoire of immediate responses (i.e. sedation, seclusion etc.). In these settings the psychiatric system is providing something of what acting out patients demand or require an early, if not immediate, response from the environment and many patients experience specialing or physical restraint as containing, since it provides a temporary relief from mental pain and feelings of insecurity. As a result, and in the short term, the patient knows where he/she stands in respect of the power or hierarchical relations within the institution. Such short-term and practical institutional reactions may also allow the staff to feel less anxious and more in control. Unwittingly, however, by providing only a symptomatic response (i.e. not exploratory of motive or consequences) they contribute to the maintenance of a status quo since thoughts or beliefs which fuel the behaviour are left untouched and unchallenged. In effect, therefore, such short-term solutions withhold from patients the opportunity of learning from experience since they do not reflect back to him or her enough of the emotional and psychological complexity of their situation, for example, that there are other people to whom to turn for care in a crisis and that they play a role in perpetuating a view of being lonely victims at the mercy of an uncaring world.

Before any psychological maturation or learning can take place, the patient's dominant unconscious emotional conflict(s) or habitual inner tension states must be remembered (i.e. experienced consciously) rather than enacted. For maturation to be achieved, therefore, the institution must indeed respond swiftly to the individual's actions but not simply to suppress or apparently deny the patients' conflicting emotional aspects, as happens when the acting out individual is construed as either the victim (especially in cases of self-harm, when the patient is closely observed by staff) or as the perpetrator (in cases of outwardly directed aggression, when the patient may be forcibly sedated or otherwise restrained). This response merely serves to collude with one or other side of the patient's internal conflict producing an interpersonal enactment, between patient and staff and/or between staff and staff who take up extreme and opposing positions, 'for' and 'against' the patient. The institution needs to provide or facilitate a wider range of responses, including genuine emotional feedback representing both sides of the patient's conflict, which is thereby tailored to the needs of the patient, allowing them to experience themselves more fully (as victim and perpetrator).  This is achieved through a connection with other people which, in summation, is responsive, supportive and empathic in the face of painful emotions.  Patients are enabled to develop psychological complexity only if they are shown, via the institutional response, a more complete and hence complex picture of themselves which supplies the hitherto denied or dismissed painful emotions or dominating unconscious dynamic theme in relation to themselves and others.  Ideally, the acting out patient experiences a swift institutional response but one which avoids behavioural extremes and delivers an empathic response.  An empathic response which conveys a range of emotional responses to the patient (which are perceived by the patient to arise out of genuine feelings since they are embedded in a relatively secure relationship) carries more therapeutic potential and containment since; (1) this avoids creating, overall, an hierarchical enactment, often of the victim-victimiser type, and (2) it allows some of the immediate anxiety, fear and excitement to be defused which allows the patient to accept and absorb verbal feedback which needs to be provided.

In many respects, entering into a treatment alliance involves, for patients, a sophisticated set of accomplishments; the ability to form a complaint; to ask for and receive help; to turn to professionals and to co-operate with what may be difficult, emotionally painful, lengthy and even unsatisfactory treatment, perhaps including incomplete symptom resolution.  Any treatment, therefore, which involves the patient in regular or prolonged treatment (as is the case of a chronic disorder such as personality disorder) is potentially problematic for patients who act out in the face of the stress of emotional conflict.

Professionals, involved with personality disordered patients who characteristically deploy such inadequately developed or infantile modes of relating (both to themselves and to others), may unwittingly enter into a style of relationship based on power and control rather than on empathy and exploration.  The task for the professional is thus to minimise an enactment of the power dynamic in relation to the patient and to facilitate an awareness in the patient of the impediments to his or her forming a straightforward treatment alliance.  Staff need to be aware of the need to facilitate engagement in treatment, rather than to take this for granted, and to be equipped with the necessary skills to achieve this. They need to convey to the patient: (1) an understanding of his or her difficulties in relating to others (especially to those in social positions of power and authority); (2) that this difficulty is based upon low self-esteem, ambivalence, fear of intimacy and basic mistrust; and (3) that these aspects may be understandable and of survival value to the patient given past experiences, although often at the cost of loneliness and a sense of profound alienation, but currently are largely maladaptive.

Successful engagement is a necessary prerequisite for successful treatment, whether psychiatric or psychotherapeutic, but, in many conventional psychiatric institutions, working with acting out patients, this necessary first stage is often not achieved. Indeed, conventional institutions by their nature can precipitate acting out behaviours. For example, Powell *et al.*, (1994) considered 931 reported incidents of violence in a 13 month period in psychiatric units. A total of 317 antecedents to the violence were identified which were features of the hospital regime and there were 165 antecedents where it was considered that actions by a staff member may possibly have contributed to the violence. Hierarchical and authoritarian arrangements are observable in all hospitals and, as argued above, they may serve to increase the likelihood of the enactment of complementary relationships victim or perpetrator based on a power differential between patients and their carers. As a result, the situation serves to maintain the status quo, since tension is discharged more readily interpersonally, between patient and staff or staff and staff, than it is contained intrapsychically by the patient and staff. For the patient, the potential for remembering rather than acting is lost and the effect is simply custodial, rather than therapeutic, containment.

Many institutions (but especially psychiatric hospitals and prisons where some of the most severely personality disordered individuals are to be found) are faced with the above difficulties: (1) effecting a sufficiently swift response to patients' acting out; (2) exerting an influence which allows an examination of antecedents and consequences, close in time to the acting out behaviour, thereby maximising new learning; (3) providing a genuine emotional response which (in total effect) is sufficiently empathic yet avoids construing the patient solely as victim or perpetrator and hence incapable of owning appropriate responsibility for the acting out behaviour; (4) providing patients with alternative outlets for psychic tension and/or with human support systems for appropriately expressed distress; and (5) creating a range of therapeutic environments which enable movement from one to another consequent upon the establishment of psychological and maturational change. Too often, a change in the patient's behaviour or attitudes is reflected by a gross (for example, discharge), absent (for example, continued admission under the same terms and conditions) or delayed institutional response (for example, when Home Office permission for discharge is required). In all the above instances, the net result is usually the absence of a creative learning experience, hence an incapacity for the individual patient to mature psychologically, to individualise.

## THE DEMOCRATIC THERAPEUTIC COMMUNITY AS AN INDIVIDUALISING INSTITUTION

An institution which combines the positive aspects of the more traditional institution (i.e., its predictable organisation and swift response to acting out) with a more thoughtful, non-complementary and wider set of responses to patients who act out, is the democratic therapeutic community, as deployed at Henderson Hospital. Henderson Hospital, through the collaborative working of residents and staff, has evolved as a hospital which serves as a "living-learning" therapeutic environment (Jones, 1953), wherein the established maladaptive attitudinal and behavioural patterns of personality disordered patients are examined and, where appropriate, abandoned for those which are more socially adaptive. In the process the patients become more themselves, i.e. they individualise. This approach, however, should not be confused with that which provides individualised treatment packages, since at Henderson all patients are subject to the same treatment programme and there are no 'key workers' or individual treatment programmes as such. On admission, Henderson Hospital patients are far from individualised (i.e. they are not individuals in the sense of knowing their own minds, being able, under ordinary circumstances, to differentiate their own thoughts, motives and feelings from those of others with whom they come into close contact, nor able to trust or depend on others in a mature fashion, i.e. to be independent). Therefore, what treatment they want is not necessarily what they need in order to mature psychologically and to individualise and, in this sense, the 'community as doctor' (Rapoport *et al.*, 1960) knows best what is required for the individual patient, who is in fact not that, i.e. not a differentiated individual, viewed psychologically.

*Peer group influence*
The task of engagement in treatment at Henderson is aided by the involvement of other patients in the interviewing process for selection of new patients, as well as in one another's subsequent treatment, including decisions concerning their discharge from the hospital. This peer group relationship, which is itself deliberately hierarchically structured, on the basis of patients' length of stay in the community (Norton, 1992), is less likely to support complementary victim or perpetrator style of relationships, since it is not buttressed by a strong staff-patient hierarchical model. This influence is achieved partly by (1) the prominence of group, as opposed to one-to-one, treatment modalities, which de-emphasise staff expertise; (2) the peer group relationships themselves, which are more horizontal than vertical, thereby maximising the potential for an empathic interaction, and (3) the fact that all treatment is voluntary, further serving to de-emphasise hierarchical or authoritarian relationships, against which the patients might otherwise tend to take up, and reinforce, a complementary, 'them and us', (vertical) position.

Selection of new patients in a group situation involving patients, who have equal voting rights to those of staff (as well as greater numbers), has the advantage that the latter are empowered to make important real decisions about their peers. This genuine empowerment recognises patients' healthy resources. The patients can challenge defensive behaviours in candidates for admission in a manner which indicates that they are not taken in by any attempt to play down or rationalise this behaviour, since many of the interviewing residents may well have similar histories or behaviours. In this they may be more effective than professionals. Whether at selection interview or subsequently during treatment such plain speaking from the peer group, to which the patient is exposed and previously unused, is less readily experienced as negative criticism since it does not emanate from a professional. An empathic relationship, albeit one which early in treatment is relatively brittle and unstable, with someone who has experienced and understands their problem from the 'inside', yields more potential for listening to and absorbing verbal feedback about the effects of acting out behaviour and suggestions for behaving (and thinking) differently in future.

*Implied treatment contract*
In being selected by their peers, Henderson patients, known as residents, voluntarily elect to forego their usual (often acting out) means of dealing with emotional conflict.   Admission is planned, in contrast to crisis admission, and the patient is aware of the implicit contract to live by the community's rules, (in particular no violence to self, others or property) which are a microcosm of those in wider society, and to actively participate in their own and others' treatment, hence the term 'resident' which avoids some of the passive connotations of 'patient'. One important result of this implicit agreement is that residents at Henderson are provided with an environment in which to experience and endure psychological tension consciously and through this to learn more adaptive ways of coping with the difficult emotions which surround the re-emerging memories, (often of chronic abuse or neglect in childhood) and which are evident once habitual acting-out solutions are prohibited.  They thus must strive to turn to the peer group for support during emotional crisis, regardless of the time of day, and to attempt to avoid their usual means of psychic tension discharge.  This involves residents in taking the risks implicit in trusting others, since human relationships cannot provide the immediate and predictable response of the bottle, the 'fix' or the (self-mutilating) blade, as in the case of Ms. Jones during the early hours.  The current relationship with staff is often perceived and experienced by residents as if that of an earlier abusive, manipulative or otherwise exploitative relationship with a previous caretaker. This distortion of current relationships is harder to maintain in the face of carers who are peers with similar histories. Ideally, the conditions created are right for residents to remember formative experiences and consciously to experience attendant emotional conflict rather than to enact it.   Only then, is the experience therapeutic, rather than custodial, containment, i.e. one which caries the potential to develop a mature, rather than an infantile, dependent style of relating, both to self and other (Fairbairn, 1952).

Inevitably new residents test out and challenge Henderson's novel, albeit "institutional", environment and they attempt to involve others (peers and staff) in an interpersonal enactment of conflict (often via violence to self, others or property) which is complementary, hence sterile in terms of learning potential. They 'bump up' against the community's rules and feel the community 'counter-punch'. Thus, inevitably complementary relationships occur but they seldom become stabilised long-term. When this does happen however, staff need to take the major responsibility for trying to unlock the projective systems, which underpin, what for example, may appear as scapegoating of a resident by his or her peers.

It is always a temptation for residents to sustain the belief that they are being maltreated and misunderstood (as victims) by an anonymous organisation. It is as if they desire to be on the receiving end of a dominating power dynamic because this is familiar to them. Anything short of this, being novel, is experienced as anxiety provoking and threatening and the accompanying anxiety and fear is not felt to be safely expressible (since there is a belief that such an appearance would betray weakness and would be exploited) therefore such feelings are masked by anger or a blank exterior which reveals nothing of the resident's internal world. Maintaining this stance, however, is harder when the institution is small (only 29 beds) and, by virtue of the prominence of the peer group influence and relaxing of the staff-patient hierarchy, also familiar and often empathic.

*Response to crisis*
The response to crisis within Henderson is often effected through the convening of an emergency meeting, called by three senior elected residents (known as 'top three'), which all residents and staff must attend. The resident in crisis needs to, for example, account for rule-breaking behaviour and its antecedents and also experience its immediate consequences, all of which are discussed and explored, there and then, or, further on in treatment, ask for support before acting out has taken place. This represents a very different situation from that which habitually attends rule breaking in wider "institutional" society when, for example, the time delay between committing a crime and being apprehended or accounting for the behaviour in a Court of Law, as well as experiencing its consequences, may be very great. In an analogous way, in hospitals, there may be an unhelpful delay in decision-making, especially when the relevant decisions are only made at the weekly ward round!

Rather than a judge and jury sitting above the rule-breaker there is, at Henderson, a peer group sitting on the same level who, nonetheless carry out a role of social censure or approval, as appropriate. At times, the residents' peer group is harshly moralistic seeming to act automatically, without reflection or empathy, to discharge one of its members and, in this way, enacting a complementary relationship. Ironically, it is the staff then who are required to act to avert an over-punitive and non-individualising response by the resident group acting upon itself, the intervention restoring a balance in the feedback by avoiding over-simplification, either victim or perpetrator. (It should be noted that the resident group has a larger say in the timing of discharge of fellow residents than does the staff group, since this is the result of a democratic, "one person one vote", system, following discussion, if a given resident is not felt to be genuinely striving to change or has broken a major rule of the community. However, there is a maximum length of stay of one year).

## Rule-breaking

At Henderson, the residents automatically discharge themselves by breaking the most important of the rules (violence to self, others or property or taking unprescribed drugs or alcohol in the hospital). However, they are able to ask the community for reinstatement, which is granted if the resident is able to convince the peer group and staff (through discussion or argument) of genuine distress, sincere regret or a commitment to future change or can provide evidence of some kind of learning from the whole experience having taken place. In this way there is a rapid response to such maladaptive behaviour (as there may be in traditional institutions) but one which is exercised predominantly by a peer group (hence horizontal) and in a more tailor-made (not 'all or nothing') manner. A mindless, automatic or else delayed decision is avoided and the potential for learning, hence individualisation, enhanced. The rule-breaking resident, however, must undergo a "re-admission" vote the next day to determine whether absolute discharge should follow. Wanting to be part, as a fully participant member, of Henderson's community, and by implication also part of society in general, serves as the ultimate motivator. Since many residents do indeed find a capacity to trust others while at Henderson they often experience a sense of belonging, to which they are unused.

That 'patients' have such a large say in the admission and discharge of fellow patients at Henderson is sometimes a cause of concern to professionals outside, particularly considering the psycho-pathological nature of the personality disordered population being treated. However, in being delegated such important decision-making in these areas the patient group is not simply construed as being as expert as trained professionals but they are credited for having areas of healthy psychological functioning as well as unhealthy parts. This is particularly so when they themselves are not immediately involved in the other's situation. Thus their antisocial behaviour is not construed as equivalent to their whole selves being anti-social. Even so, the manipulating, intimidating, seducing or scapegoating of a fellow resident remain ever-present risks and staff are often required to interpret the resident group's vindictive and automatic (complementary) response in wishing impulsively to expel an individual community member. In this way experience over nearly 50 years at Henderson has built in some safeguards such as a cooling off period of 24 hours between the rule breaking incident and the final 're-admission' vote but not with the loss of immediate feedback.

The culture of immediate exploration, via emergency meetings of the whole community, to try to understand the aberrant or maladaptive behaviour (which usually is more evident during the informal, unstructured part of the day) allows issues to be discussed and explored within the group setting of the whole community and gradually acting-out behaviour can be ameliorated through this process. Indeed some residents have faced (and survived) as many as twenty "discharge" votes in their one year admission to Henderson, their acting-out behaviour taking on less extreme forms commensurate with an increase in verbal articulation of upset feelings to their peers with time spent living in the community. It is clear that once the community has reached a stage where the majority of its members no longer accept a resident then that person's position becomes increasingly untenable, since little useful treatment can result and, indeed, harm can ensue were the stay prolonged. However, it is unusual for a resident to be discharged solely by dint of the residents' larger 'block' vote and staff are keenly aware of the amount of power residing in the residents' group but also that they and the residents are mutually dependent upon one another in order to keep the community therapeutic.

Despite the delegation of important clinical decision-making at Henderson to the whole community, the medical and non-medical staff retain conventional professional role responsibilities, as in other hospitals. Unsurprisingly, the legal issues in relation to medical negligence are raised by some as an objection to this method of working. However, it is clear that the courts will not find a doctor negligent if he or she acts in a way accepted at the time by a responsible body of medical opinion even though others adopt a different practice Bolam v Friern Hospital Management Committee [1957] 1 WLR 582,. Although a 'responsible body of medical opinion' remains undefined, it is established, in Maynard v W. Midlands R.H.A. [1985] 1 All ER 635 (HL), that it is not sufficient to show that there is a body of competent professional opinion which believes the practice is wrong if there is a body which supports the practice in reasonable circumstances, even if that 'body' is a very small number of practitioners Defreitas v O'Brien [1995] Feb 16th Times LR. The professionals who have referred their patients to the Hospital over the years implicitly endorse these admission and discharge procedures as part and parcel of a treatment which, for those who stay seven months or more, is successful in 71 per cent of cases no further re-conviction or hospitalisation in three years post-discharge (Whiteley, 1970; Copas *et al.*, 1984). Thus, although the decision-making process at Henderson Hospital may not be that used or preferred by all psychiatrists or institutions, it seems unlikely that it could be considered negligent.

## IMPLICATIONS FOR 'NON-DEMOCRATIC' AND NON-SPECIALIST HOSPITALS

Clearly, the structure and culture which has evolved at Henderson is not appropriate to every therapeutic setting and, how far the model can be generalised is not known, although democratic therapeutic communities have been set up in many different hospital, prison and educational settings, including some which employ compulsory detention in maximum security (Abruzzi, 1975; Clarke and Glatt, 1985; Cullen, 1994; Feldbrugge, 1992; Ogloff, Wong and Greenwood, 1990; Ravndal & Vaglum, 1991; Vaglum *et al*, 1990). The nature of the institution in question will have an important bearing on how much of, and how far, the Henderson democratic therapeutic community model might be appropriately utilised in connection with responding to acting-out behaviour. However, some lessons concerning the institutional management of personality disordered people who act out are reasonably clear and should not now need to be repeatedly learned (and forgotten) by successive generations of the professionals, who, incidentally, also find it hard to learn from experience, including from that of their fellow professionals!

*What has been learned?*
In a residential setting, the clinical experience is often that a *homogeneous population* of personality disordered individuals is more successfully treated, given a structured therapeutic environment, such as at Henderson or Grendon Underwood Prison, than is a smaller number of personality disordered patients in a heterogeneous (for example, acute or long-stay) psychiatric ward which is not so structured or rich in terms of an active treatment model nor consistent in its application.   The disproportionate demand for staff time and the curtailment of a ward's activities in the face of a single acting out patient is well known (see Miller for a review of in-patient treatment of 'borderline patients' Miller, 1989)

What is required, through the necessary internal organisation of the institution, is a setting in which acting-out patients are enabled to support and educate one another (at least to some degree) and, in that sense, develop psychosocially through more *horizontal relationships* with peers and staff rather than to have reinforced authoritarian (vertical) relationships which only serve to elicit and promote oppositional, anti-authority and complementary behaviour and relationships.  This ideal is harder to achieve as the need for custodial security increases, however, failure to obviate the patient's need to act out often leads to a perceived need by staff to increase the level of security of accommodation.

What is also crucial, in order to avoid non-therapeutic hierarchical structures which may result from static populations of patients (or inmates), is that genuine progress from infantile towards mature dependence, i.e. increased psychological maturity, is responded to by an *appropriately timed and paced move*, when necessary, to a different environment in terms of the level of psychological maturity required by it (as in a move from a locked to an open facility).

There is also a need for a *range of articulated environments*, for patients of different levels of psychological maturity, between which they can move as clinically (psychologically and behaviourally) dictated and not subject to the time delays, for example, of a remote Home Office as in the case of certain detained patients.   Many of the existing traditional institutions function so as to provide patients with abrupt environmental transitions in terms of timing or of degree of psychological maturity required, for which they cannot be adequately prepared and in which they cannot function adaptively (especially if the demands of the new are too high i.e. not 'articulated' to the old).   In this way earlier psychological traumata associated with separation and loss are repeated in treatment or custodial settings and, again, without the possibility of learning from the traumatising experience.   Attention must be paid to the psychological preparation of the individual for any such move so that attendant emotions can be integrated with the event, leaving time to say a proper 'goodbye'.   This is particularly the case if it is known that the 'gap' between environments is large (in terms of the psychological maturity required of the patient to survive and flourish in it) as, for example, between in-patient and day-patient or between day-patient and out-patient settings.

There is a need, as far as possible, for all staff involved in the treatment setting to agree *a single treatment approach* (if not a formal treatment contract) for a given patient or, at least, to discuss openly amongst themselves their differences of opinion so that these do not remain covert. This is much easier when dealing with a homogeneous patient group and when there is only one treatment approach as in the democratic style therapeutic community.   Even then, however, the acting out patient group exert pressure on staff to respond with an authoritarian style and to become involved in power-based rather than empathic relationships, resulting in therapeutic staff being experienced as malicious 'prison warders', hence, in the minds of residents, punitive, alien and untrustworthy.   Professionals may be, in effect, set against one another by the provocative behaviour of their charges who, on the one hand, elicit sympathy and understanding (as victim) and, on the other, evoke a punitive response (as perpetrator of rule-breaking via acting out behaviour).   Importantly, more adaptive coping strategies or support must be offered to patients if they are to stop discharging emotional conflicts via acting-out.

Staff need to be aware of the nature of the pressures exerted on them by such patients and to be able to construct their own means of mutual support and self-examination in order to minimise the effects of the divisive and polarising "splitting" mechanisms, as above. Staff groups also need to be empowered with greater responsibility and accountability for the discharge and transfer of those in their care. Only in this way can they be enabled to maintain their own capacity for mature dependence (rather than infantile dependence within an hierarchical structure) in a way which acts as a role model for patients, who are thereby, potentially, enabled to develop their own capacities for maturation and individualisation.

## CONCLUSIONS

All healthcare institutions are exposed to acting-out behaviour and have developed cultures and systems by which such occurrences are dealt with, to varying degrees of success, in terms of the patient's individualisation. Obviously not all institutions will need, or be able, to completely adopt a democratic therapeutic community approach with the potential advantages described above. Some principles of this model, however, in relation to a personality disordered clientele, may be applicable to other institutions which operate at different levels of security or in less specialist settings.

Some of the points described and discussed above can be translated to a range of settings and particularly an awareness of the interaction between the individual and the 'institution', and of the often complementary style of this interaction, may empower professionals working in institutions to break the therapeutic stalemate. However, to achieve this requires changes in attitudes and behaviour on the part of staff and some restructuring of the internal organisation of the institution so as to influence both staff-staff and staff-patient relationships, with the main objective of facilitating alternative adaptive methods of discharging or expressing psychic distress. Staff training in the above issues discussed in this paper, along with their mutual and continuing support and supervision, are essential in providing a culture in which such relationships can develop.

# REFERENCES

ABRUZZI, W., (1975) Severe personality disorders in an institutional setting. *American Journal of Psychoanalysis,* pp 269-77.

AQUILINA, C. (1991) Violence by psychiatric in-patients *Medicine Science and the Law,* 31(4), pp 306-312.

CLARKE, C.R., GLATT, M.M., (1985) Wormwood Scrubs annexe a therapeutic community within a prison: discussion paper, *Journal of the Royal Society of Medicine,* 78, pp 656-62.

COPAS, J.B., O'BRIEN, M., ROBERTS, J. & WHITELEY, S. (1984) Treatment outcome in personality disorder: The effect of social, psychological and behavioural variables. *Personality and Individual Differences* 5(5), pp 565-573.

CROCKET, R. (1966) Acting-out as a mode of communication in the Psychotherapeutic Community *British Journal of Psychiatry.* 112, pp 383-383.

CULLEN, E. (1994) Grendon: The therapeutic prison that works *Therapeutic Communities* Vol. 15(4), pp 301-311.

DOLAN, B.M., COID, J. (1993) *Psychopathic and Antisocial Personality Disorders: Treatment And Research Issues,* Gaskell, London.

FAIRBAIRN, W.R.D. (1952) *Psychoanalytic studies of the personality.* London: Routledge and Kegan Paul.

FELDBRUGGE, J.T. (1992), Rehabilitation of patients with personality disorders: patient-staff collaboration used as a working model and a tool, *Criminal Behaviour and Mental Health* 2, pp 169-177.

HEALTH AND SAFETY COMMISSION (1987) *Violence to Staff in the Health Services* Health Services Advisory Committee, HMSO, London.

H.M.PRISON SERVICE (1993) *Corporate Plan 1993-6.* London, H.M.Prison Service.

JONES, M. (1953) *The therapeutic community: a new treatment method in psychiatry.* New York: Basic Books.

LAPLANCHE, J. PONTALIS, J.-B. (1983) *The language of psychoanalysis.* London: The Hogarth Press and the Institute of Psychoanalysis.

MASTERSON, J.F. (1972) *Treatment of the borderline adolescent: A developmental approach* New York, Wiley

MILLER, L.J., (1989) Inpatient management of borderline personality disorder: A review and update, *Journal of Personality Disorders,* 3(2), pp 122-134.

NORTON, K.R.W. (1992) Personality disordered individuals: the Henderson Hospital model of treatment. *Criminal Behaviour and Mental Health* 2, pp 180-191.

OGLOFF, J.R.P., WONG, S., GREENWOOD, A., (1990) Treating criminal psychopaths in a therapeutic community program, *Behavioral Sciences and the Law,* 8, pp 181-90.

POWELL, G., CAAN, W., CROWE, M. (1994) What events precede violent incidents in psychiatric hospitals? *British Journal of Psychiatry.* 165, pp 107-112.

RAPOPORT, R. (1960) *Community as Doctor* Tavistock, London

RAVNDAL, E. VAGLUM, P. (1991) Changes in antisocial aggressiveness during treatment in a hierarchical therapeutic community. A prospective study of personality Changes. *Acta Psychiatrica Scandinavica*, 84(6), pp 524-30.

REED, J. (1994) *Report on joint Department of Health/Home Office committee on services for mentally disordered offenders and others requiring similar services.* HMSO, London.

THOMAS, C., BARTLETT, A.E. MEZEY, G. (1995) The extent and effects of violence amongst psychiatric in-patients *Psychiatric Bulletin* in press.

VAGLUM, P., FRIIS, S., IRION, T., JOHNS, S., KARTERUD, S., LARSEN, F., VAGLUM, S. (1990), Treatment response of severe and non-severe personality disorders in a therapeutic community day unit, *Journal of Personality Disorders,* 4(2), pp 161-72.

WHITELEY, JS (1970) The response of psychopaths to a therapeutic community *British Journal of Psychiatry* 116, pp 517-529.

# Treatment Outcome in Personality Disorder
## The Effect of Social, Psychological and Behavioural Variables

John Copas, Maja O'Brien, Joanna Roberts & Stuart Whiteley

**Personality and Individual Differences**
*1984, Vol. 5(5): pp 565-573*

The study followed up 245 patients referred to the Henderson Hospital (194 admitted for treatment and 51 not admitted) and for whom information had been collected on their social background and certain psychological variables allowing a classification and typology of personality disorder to be worked out. The study indicates that the therapeutic community treatment is effective with selected individuals showing the antisocial behaviour associated with such disorder. In particular this treatment is of benefit to the offenders with only one conviction and who are able to persevere with treatment for a period of 6 months for treatment to be maximally effective. The variation of psychological types within the broad category of personality disorder was demonstrated and this has a bearing on the outcome of treatment, the extrapunitive neurotic being of poorest prognosis with or without treatment. Yet even in this group, therapeutic community treatment can be effective.

## INTRODUCTION

The purpose of the study was to examine the relationship of treatment outcome to a variety of individual measures in patients diagnosed as having a psychopathic or personality disorder. The factors included social history features, personality factors and psychological type and length of stay. The first part of the paper summarises part of the original investigation by O'Brien (1976), in which a psychological typology of personality disorder was devised and tested against the observed patterns of previous social maladjustment. The second part of the study deals with the follow-up of cases from the sample and the statistical analysis of the findings. Thus, overall, the study provides an interesting comparison with previous Henderson Hospital follow-up studies (Whiteley, 1970; Copas and Whiteley, 1976) whilst increasing the range of information gathered and extending the group studied to include women and those not admitted for treatment. It was hoped that the results from this investigation would contribute to a better understanding of which patients responded well to treatment and so aid selection of suitable candidates for treatment by the therapeutic community method as has been practised at Henderson Hospital for many years. For a detailed description of the method of treatment, the reader is referred to other sources (Whiteley, Briggs and Turner, 1972).

## THE BACKGROUND STUDY

*Social history features*
The individuals in the original sample (O'Brien, 1976) showed several signs of maladjustment generally associated with the diagnosis of psychopathic disorder or personality disorder, and were largely referred with the diagnostic label of psychopath, personality disorder, sociopath etc.

A substantial number had been previously convicted and although the number of female patients convicted of criminal offences was smaller than that of the males, when the groups were compared with the general population, the females showed a greater incidence of delinquency than the males. The sample also had a high proportion of subjects with previous psychiatric admissions. There was a much smaller proportion of married people than would be found in a similar age group in the general population, and among this group there was an abnormally high level of divorce and separation. When compared with previous samples (Whiteley, 1970) these characteristics appear to have remained fairly constant, except that the present sample showed a lower proportion of those with previous criminal convictions and a higher incidence of those with previous psychiatric admission than in former studies, and this might be a consequence of a more positive selection policy resulting from experience gained in the previous studies.


*Psychological assessment*

The following three psychometric tests were sent to the candidate by post for completion prior to the selection interview: the Hostility and Direction of Hostility Questionnaire (HDHQ; Foulds, 1965); the S-R Inventory of Anxiousness (SRIA; Endler, Hunt and Rosenstein, 1962) with modifications by one of the present authors (O'Brien, 1976); the Ego Identity Scale (EIS; Rasmussen, 1964) with additional items from the Eysenck Personality Inventory Lie Scale (Eysenck and Eysenck, 1964).   The results of the psychological tests are discussed in detail in O'Brien (1976) and are summarised here (see Table 5).

The sample showed an average *Hostility* (H) score that was higher than that obtained by any other abnormal group in the original study, including the psychotic group.   The presence of hostility or aggression in groups diagnosed as psychopathic, or personality disordered, is usually referred to either directly or indirectly in clinical definitions of the disorder, through observations on the characteristic antisocial and sometimes violent behaviour.   The group also showed a mean *Ego identity* score which was significantly lower than that for normal control subjects, indicating poor psycho-social adjustment and ego diffusion, consistent with definitions of psychopathic or personality disorders.   However, the sample had a higher level of anxiety than the control subjects and a tendency towards *intropunitiveness* which was inconsistent with the conventional view of the true psychopath, as outlined by Cleckley (1964).   It is partly as a result of these latter inconsistencies that it was suggested by O'Brien (1976) that the diagnostic category of psychopathic personality may be more appropriately applied to only a subgroup of the category of personality disorder and that further research in this field should attempt to identify personality differences within this broad category.   In such an attempt a measure of anxiety and direction of hostility would be two dimensions for further study.

The O'Brien (1976) study prompted the formulation of a typology using the findings on two psychometric tests, the SRIA and the HDHQ.   A median value was computed separately for the males and the females and the model then proposed by O'Brien expresses anxiety in terms of higher and lower values and the direction of hostility in terms of a continuum between extrapunitiveness and intropunitiveness as follows:

(i) *Neurotic* (N), showing high anxiety and intropunitiveness;
(ii) *Extrapunitive Neurotic* (EN), showing high anxiety and extrapunitiveness;
(iii) *Intropunitive Psychopath* (IP), showing intropunitiveness and low anxiety;
(iv) *Psychopath* (P), showing low anxiety and extrapunitiveness

The validity of the proposed model was then tested by O'Brien by analysing to what extent the subjects so classified displayed expected differences in social behaviour, as measured by the incidence of a previous criminal or psychiatric history.

The main hypothesis tested was that different personality types within a sample of individuals with personality disorders would show differences in modes of socially maladjusted behaviour, i.e. in the predominance of a past record of criminal behaviour or of psychiatric hospital admission. These differences would be most pronounced between the N and the P groups, the so-called 'pure' groups. The neurotic subjects would have a predominantly psychiatric record whilst the psychopathic subjects would have a predominantly criminal record. The so-called 'mixed' groups, the EN and the IP groups, would not show a clear tendency towards either a psychiatric or a criminal history.

The relationship between personality type and the incidence of past adult criminal and psychiatric history was tested by means of a $\chi^2$ test and found to be statistically significant at the $p < 0.001$ level. The results supported the expectation that the interaction between personality dimensions of anxiety and the direction of hostility is strongly associated with differences in social maladjustment and thus suggested that the model proposed for the classification of this category of psychiatric disorder was valid and may provide a useful approach in trying to clarify the diagnostic confusion in this area.

## THE FOLLOW-UP STUDY

The sample followed-up consisted of 235 individuals (male and female) from the O'Brien sample who had been referred to the Henderson Hospital between September 1969 and February 1971 for assessment interviews with a view to admission. There were 169 males and 76 females with a mean age of 26.5 years ranging from 17 to 39 years; 72% were unmarried, a further 10% were divorced and separated and 18% were still married at the time of interview.

Not all the subjects completed the personality tests necessary for psychological typing. Of those subsequently admitted 147 completed the tests but for general outcome purposes all the subjects (194) were followed-up. Approx. 30% of all those who were referred but not admitted did complete sufficient tests to be psychologically typed and these cases (51) were included in the study.

The reasons for non-admission were various, e.g. failure to attend the interview (17), rejection as unsuitable after interview (25), failure to attend for admission or another course intervening, e.g. imprisonment or hospitalisation elsewhere (9).

Information pertaining to criminal convictions and psychiatric hospital admission prior to the present referral was ascertained for each subject from the Criminal Records Office and the Department of Health and Social Security, respectively.

Certain key social maladjustment features, namely, a history of juvenile convictions, admission to Approved School, convictions as an adult and previous admissions to a psychiatric hospital and the basic psychological test scores for both the admitted and the not-admitted group were compared and did not differ significantly. Table 1 illustrates the distribution of those cases from the admitted and not-admitted groups between the four psychological types and also the incidence of previous criminal history or psychiatric hospital admission.

## METHODOLOGY

The subsequent careers of the subjects in the sample were followed-up over periods of 3 and 5 years after discharge from Henderson Hospital following a period of treatment or over the same periods following the date of an assessment interview after which they had not been admitted for treatment. (The details of subsequent criminal convictions and/or subsequent psychiatric hospital admissions were again ascertained from the Criminal Records Office and the Department of Health and Social Security, respectively). As in the previous follow-up studies (Whiteley, 1970; Copas and Whiteley, 1976), failure was taken to be a further conviction and/or a further psychiatric hospital admission if the period under survey.

Those subjects for whom no information on further convictions nor hospital admissions were recorded (i.e. the success group, $n = 64$), and for whom the hospital had had no further information from other sources, were followed-up through the National Health Central Register to ensure that they had not died or emigrated, but no such causes for absence were discovered in this group for the time period under study.

In addition to the allocation to a psychological type, information on social history factors such as sex, marital status, delinquency and psychiatric history had been collected and length of stay in treatment was recorded for those admitted. Although the not-admitted group cannot be deemed a control group it was nonetheless analysed separately and can still serve as a comparative group and an indication as to the outcome of those not treated at Henderson Hospital.

**Table 1.**

**Psychological Type and Previous Maladjustment**

| GROUP | Psychological Type | | | | Total |
|---|---|---|---|---|---|
| | N | EN | IP | P | |
| Admitted | 40 | 34 | 36 | 37 | 147 |
| Not admitted | 19 | 12 | 12 | 8 | 51 |
| **TOTAL** | **59** | **46** | **48** | **45** | **198** |
| With juvenile convictions | 15% | 22% | 17% | 38% | |
| With adult convictions | 47% | 52% | 50% | 76% | |
| With previous psychiatric admission | 78% | 76% | 67% | 38% | |

*Statistical method of data analysis*

The extensive statistical analysis of the data was carried out by Copas. The substantial amount of data available for each patient was first coded and edited into a consistent form on a computer file. The preliminary stage of the analysis consisted of examining tabulations and cross-tabulations of the variables and the correlation between them. This isolated those factors which were likely to be of interest in  particular those which might be of value in predicting outcome. An overall picture of how the variables correlate with outcome was built up using several different methods.

(a) The sample was divided into two groups, those with a successful outcome and those who had failed according to the criterion defined earlier. Significance of the individual variables could then be assessed by comparing one group with the other. This was also done separately for each of the four personality types.

(b) The association between an individual characteristic and outcome is best described by calculating a 'relative risk' as follows (Everitt, 1977):

$$R = \text{relative risk} = \frac{\text{success rate (treated) x failure rate (untreated)}}{\text{failure rate (treated) x success rate (untreated)}}$$

The characteristic has been taken in terms of a 'treated' group and an 'untreated' group, $R$ being the increase in odds on success for the treated group as compared with the untreated group. The larger is $R$, the better is the treatment; $R = 1$ denoting a zero effect, a value of $R < 1$ meaning that the treatment actually makes the success rate worse.

(c) Where the simultaneous effect of several variables is concerned, the techniques of multiple regression, discriminant analysis and the 'logistic regression' method, as used in Copas and Whiteley (1976) were used.  By these means it is possible to test whether the association between a particular factor and outcome might be explained in terms of differences on one or more of the other variables.

(d) The graphical method of Copas (1983) was used to investigate the dependence of success rate on different values of each of the quantitative variables, for example, the length of stay in hospital.

The results of using these methods on the data gave rise to a large number of tables and figures which are only briefly summarised in this paper. It is well known that some caution is needed in interpreting the significance levels achieved in a study of this kind, since with so many factors under consideration a small number of apparently significant effects are likely to arise purely by chance. A further fact is that there can be no natural control group for the Henderson patients and so the correlations in themselves do not necessarily imply a causative effect.

## RESULTS

On the criteria stated, the overall success rates for patients in he sample who were admitted to the therapeutic community at Henderson Hospital was 41% at the 3 year follow up compared with 23% in the not-admitted group, with a fall to 36% in the 5 year follow up compared with 19% in the not-admitted group (Table 2). Various factors were examined in relation to success by the statistical methods alluded to above.

A logistic regression was completed, as in the earlier study, on predictive factors (Copas and Whiteley, 1976) which related success to sex, age, length of stay and psychological type and the possible interaction between them. This demonstrated that the effect of sex on outcome was negligible with the success rates for males at 3 years being 36% and 32% at 5 years, and for females 38% at 3 years and 34% at 5 years. Age also appeared to have little bearing. At the 3 year mark the average age of the successful was 26.4 years, and of the failed 26.6 years. At 5 years the average age of the successful group was 26.6 years, and for the failed group 26.5 years. *Marital status* was also screened but did not appear to affect the outcome.

**Table 2**

**Success rate by 4-week periods.**

| | Not admitted | Length of stay in months | | | | | | | | Total Admitted |
|---|---|---|---|---|---|---|---|---|---|---|
| | | 0-1 | 1-2 | 2-3 | 3-4 | 4-5 | 5-6 | 6-9 | 9+ | |
| %Success 3 yrs | 23 | 29 | 34 | 36 | 32 | 44 | 43 | 62 | 71 | 41% |
| % Success 5 yrs | 19 | 22 | 31 | 32 | 26 | 44 | 43 | 57 | 65 | 36% |
| *No. of cases* | *51* | *51* | *29* | *25* | *19* | *18* | *14* | *21* | *17* | *194* |

*Length of stay*
As shown in Table 2, there was a steady improvement in success rate when correlated with increasing length of stay. When the percentage success rate was plotted against the length of stay for each patient (Copas, 1983), results showed a consistent rise (Figure 1).

**Figure 1.**

**Success rate (%) plotted against number of weeks in hospital for 3 and 5 year follow-up**

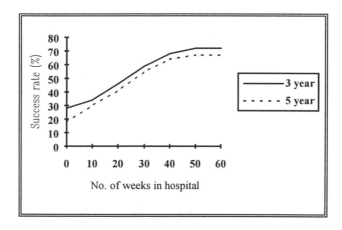

*Social background factors*
Detailed analysis of some key social history variables, already alluded to, showed few differences between the admitted and the not-admitted group. Social history factors may be associated with how long an individual remains in treatment, however. Thus, although 23% of those admitted and 24% of those not admitted had a history of *juvenile convictions*, 33% of those leaving before 17 days had a history of juvenile convictions, whereas of those who stayed over 165 days only 13% had such. Other social background factors and their relationship to outcome were examined by calculating the 'relative risk' for each factor, as outlined earlier. Those leaving before 17 days were excluded for the purpose of this calculation; 17 days is the period spent in the New Residents introductory group. The

Table 3

Outcome in relation to social factors and length of stay

% success at 3 years (no. of cases)

| Factor | Freq. | Not Admitted | Length of stay (days) | | Total Admitted | R |
|---|---|---|---|---|---|---|
| | | | 1-17 | 18+ | | |
| Juvenile Convictions | None | 26 (39) | 31 (32) | 48 (117) | 44(149) | 2.6 |
| | 1+ | 17 (12) | 19 (16) | 34 (29) | 29 (45) | 2.5 |
| Approved School | Yes | 0 (5) | 25 (4) | 17 (12) | 19 (16) | - |
| | No | 26 (46) | 27 (44) | 48 (134) | 43 (178) | 2.6 |
| Adult Convictions | 0 | 41 (22) | 31 (26) | 55 (65) | 48 (1) | 1.8 |
| | 1 | 17 (6) | 22 (9) | 52 (31) | 45 (40) | 5.3 |
| | 2+ | 9 (23) | 23 (13) | 28 (50) | 27 (63) | 3.9 |

outcome in relation to social factors and length of stay and the 'relative risk' for each factor is shown in Table 3.

Thus, of those with one conviction, only 17% were successful from the not-admitted group after 3 years as opposed to 52% from those admitted and who stayed over 18 days, giving an R value of 5.3. For those with no convictions, the R value is not so high (R = 1.8) and there was a 41% success rate in the not-admitted and a 55% success rate in those who were admitted and stayed over 18 days. The smaller disparity indicates they are a 7group 'less at risk' without treatment and for whom, therefore, treatment is not as dramatically successful.

*Psychological type and outcome*
The major part of the follow-up study was the examination of the effect of psychological type on outcome, which is shown in Table 4.

**Table 4.**

### Psychological Type and Outcome
### % success (no. of cases)

| Psychological Type | Not admitted | Length of stay (days) | | All admitted | R |
|:---:|:---:|:---:|:---:|:---:|:---:|
| | | 1- 17 | 18+ | | |
| N | 32 (19) | 33 (9) | 52 (31) | 48 (40) | 2.3 |
| | 26 (19) | 22 (9) | 45 (31) | 40 (40) | 2.3 |
| EN | 8 (12) | 18 (11) | 35 (23) | 29 (34) | 6.2 |
| | 0 (12) | 9 (11) | 35 (23) | 26 (34) | - |
| IP | 25 (12) | 33 (9) | 48 (27) | 44 (36) | 2.8 |
| | 25 (12) | 22 (9) | 44 (27) | 39 (36) | 2.4 |
| P | 25 (8) | 29 (7) | 53 (30) | 49 (37) | 3.4 |
| | 25 (8) | 29 (7) | 50 (30) | 46 (37) | 3.0 |

* *The upper row in each column represents 3 year data, the lower row 5 year data*

The success rates at the follow-up for the N, P and IP groups were similar, whereas there was a somewhat lower success rate for the EN group. When the outcome for those of the not-admitted group who had been sampled was considered, the EN group showed a particularly low success rate, although numbers were small and conclusions must be guarded. The 'relative risk' was calculated for these subgroups and showed that the EN group had the highest value (R = 6.2). This indicates that, although this group had the poorest outcome prognosis, the disparity between those treated and those untreated is more pronounced than for any other group, which suggests that treatment is effective.

Close analysis of the groups was made using multiple regression to see whether the poor prognosis for the EN group could be explained by some of the social history factors or length of stay. The values of the variance ratio (F) resulting from this multiple-regression study remained almost unchanged when the other factors (previous convictions, previous psychiatric admissions, length of stay) were allowed for, suggesting that the EN classification is an independent indicator of failure and not a mere consequence of the differing profiles over the background factors. At a simpler level, when cases were broken down into those who had previous convictions and those who had not, and similarly using juvenile convictions and previous psychiatric admissions, the EN cases continued to have the lowest success rate of the four psychological types.

*Personality variables*
The psychological test scores at initial assessment for both the admitted and the not-admitted group were compared and, as with the social history features, did not differ significantly, although certain trends were discernible over the period of time spent in treatment.

The means for H are high in all the subdivisions but those who fail after 165 days are those with the highest levels of hostility. The mean Direction of Hostility (DH score was highest (indicating intropunitiveness) in the not-admitted group (+ 3.3) and lowest in the group staying in treatment over 28 days (+ 1.7) but as can be seen from the outcome results, a lower score (indicating a lesser degree of intropunitiveness) is related to failure in those who stayed over 165 days. The successful have a tendency toward intropunitiveness without being extreme.

**Table 5**

**Psychological variables, length of stay and outcome**

| Variable (mean score) | Not Admitted | Length of stay (days) | | Total admitted | Outcome at 165+ days | |
|---|---|---|---|---|---|---|
| | | 1-17 | 18 + | | Success* | Failure* |
| **EIS score** | 69.5 | 69.5 | 67.3 | 67.8 | 68.7 70.3 | 59.1 57.1 |
| **SRIA score** | 220 | 231 | 214 | 218 | 216 217 | 225 219 |
| **HDHQ H score** | 30.1 | 29.6 | 32.1 | 31.5 | 30.9 30.5 | 34.8 34.6 |
| **HDHQ DH score** | +3.3 | +2.9 | +1.7 | +2.0 | +3.0 +2.9 | +1.6 +1.9 |

* *The upper row in the last two columns represents 3 year data, the lower row 5 year data*

The mean EIS score is relatively constant in the various subdivisions in Table 5, being 69.5 for the not-admitted and 67.8 for the admitted, but there is a difference in the outcome column when we consider those who stayed over 165 days. The successful group (at 5 year. follow-up) score 70.3 and the failures 57.1 which indicates that those with a more established ego structure are more likely to benefit from the treatment than those with poor ego structure. The mean scores on the SRIA show little change across the subdivisions; those with the highest level of anxiety leave early in treatment.

## DISCUSSION

Previous researchers have tried to design controlled studies at Henderson Hospital but found the methodological, administrative and ethical problems too daunting and there is in any case a move away from such classicism in sociological surveys (Manning, 1979). The problems of constructing and carrying out a controlled evaluation of a therapeutic community have been well described by Clarke and Cornish (1972).

The not-admitted group in the present study, although not a control group, does provide an interesting group for comparison and is particularly pertinent as there are few differences with regard to social background, personality variables or personality type between the admitted and not-admitted groups. Obviously the not-admitted group are to some extent a self-selected group in that they did complete and return the personality tests prior to the selection interview and only comprise 30% of those who were subsequently not admitted. However, the fact that they did co-operate and complete the tests might be considered an indication of positive motivation which makes them more meaningful as a comparative group.

In general, the study showed that the subjects referred to Henderson Hospital were largely regarded by outside referral agencies as falling within the diagnostic category of psychopathic disorder, personality disorder or similar. The degree and type of antisocial behaviour displayed was consistent with this categorisation, but the psychological findings demonstrated a variety of findings within the sample rather than the consistent picture of the extrapunitive, anxiety-free individual which is the classic description of the psychopath (Cleckley, 1964). There was a spread between extrapunitive and intropunitive personalities but a general bias toward intropunitiveness and a tendency towards higher anxiety within this sample which had been selected by the referral sources for possible treatment in hospital rather than management by other means. The view of psychopathy as being divided into two groups, primary and secondary, depending on the absence or not of anxiety is one that has already been described and has support in clinical practice (Karpmann, 1947; Hare, 1970).

The overall results of the treatment, which is a relatively consistent approach using the therapeutic community method, suggest that the treatment is effective in this difficult patient group but that time is required for benefit to accrue. There is little difference in outcome between those not admitted and those who leave within the first 4 weeks (23 and 29%, respectively) but a steady improvement occurs with increasing time spent in treatment, up to a 71% success rate for those staying 9 months or more and a 41% success rate overall.

The successful outcome in the present study is similar to the 40.1% non-relapse reported in the previous study of male subjects (Whiteley, 1970) and the 41% success rate after 1 year reported by Rapoport (1960).

Previous studies have indicated that those who benefited from Henderson Hospital were those who are less disturbed, have some personality and relationship resources and can regress moderately in treatment, particularly over a 6 month stay. Aggressive personalities do badly with extreme acting-out behaviour are also not responsive and some can be further traumatised by the intensified social stresses in the treatment (Rapoport, 1960). Another study demonstrated that those males who had shown some evidence of achievement at school, in occupation and by forming a marital relationship at some time and had an 'affective' or feeling personality would be more likely to benefit (Whiteley, 1970). In a further study of behavioural and attitudinal changes in Henderson patients, compared with groups in a Detention Centre and an After-care Hostel and using a Repertory Grid method, the Henderson group were shown to gain most in self-esteem during the course of treatment and to become more independent and aspire towards less rule-breaking behaviour. The effects were most marked after a stay of 6 months (Norris, 1983). Low or falling esteem is associated with delinquent behaviour.

The present study allowed the relationship of outcome to some of the social history and personality variables to be examined. The group with one previous conviction had a high value for 'relative risk' (R = 5.3), indicting a marked disparity in successful outcome between the treated and the untreated.

Some benefit could be demonstrated in all the four psychological types but the EN group proposes a particular problem for the treaters. On the one hand this is the group of poorest prognosis (both treated and untreated) and perhaps is most similar to the group which Eysenck (1970) has described with a combination of Extroversion and Neuroticism and at least likely to respond to conditioning treatment or socialising influences. On the other hand, the differences in outcome between those treated and those untreated in the EN group is marked with a high value for the 'relative risk' factor (R = 6.2), indicating that a treatment intervention of this type can be effective relative to the low level of expectation for this group.

From the psychological assessments it seems that although both of Karpmann's (1947) psychopathic types will be encountered in the sample, there is a preponderance of secondary psychopaths with a high level of anxiety and intropunitiveness, which is what one might expect in a group referred to a psychiatric hospital for treatment and is consistent with previous studies on hospitalised psychopaths (Foulds, Caine and Creasy, 1960; Marks, 1965). With such individuals, treatment will be aimed at lessening the pathological anxiety and helping them to cope in a more realistic and less 'acting-out' way whilst for the primary psychopath, treatment is aimed at promoting a reasonable level of social anxiety by confronting them with the consequences of their behaviour.

Many of the findings in the present study were confirmed in recent work by Gudjonsson and Roberts (1982), which showed that patients admitted to Henderson Hospital tended to exhibit very high levels of anxiety, had poorly socialised personality characteristics (lacking role-taking ability and high on impulsiveness), poor self-concepts and reported a preoccupation with feelings of guilt, subjective and electrodermal measures and the non-specific guilt levels illustrated in the study (Gudjonsson and Roberts, 1982) underline the need not only to relieve the high anxiety levels but also to concentrate on increasing emotional and bodily awareness and to encourage guilt and anxiety to be more situationally specific.

*Behaviour during treatment*
Some behavioural observations made during treatment are worthy of comment. There was a significant difference in the rate of rule-breaking

between those who obtained a successful outcome and those who failed (P < 0.05), with the failures breaking about 50% more rules on average than the successes. Those who ultimately failed also tended to be those whose rule-breaking increased during treatment. A discharge by community vote early in treatment was also associated with failure. Clearly these aspects demonstrate the imperviousness of the individual to peer-group pressures. However, a discharge by community vote at a late stage in treatment was not so linked to poor outcome and it may well be that an individual who has made some progress, yet cannot bring himself to terminate treatment in a planned way, sets up the situation in which he faces a community discharge. Thus, for those who stayed 165 days or more the success rate was substantially better: a 50% success rate for those discharged by the community compared with a 70% success rate for those leaving normally. Although the numbers are small, this result suggests that this type of discharge, at this stage, is more likely to be a neurotic device on the part of the individual to end treatment, rather than a rejection of the community's rules and values, and therefore has a less negative connotation.

A group of patients who had a particularly poor outcome were those who were solely violent to themselves, through self-mutilation and other forms of self-damage. This group only had a 23% success rate at 3 year follow up. Those who showed external violence or a combination of external violence and violence to self, showed similar success rates (42 and 45% respectively) to those who demonstrated no violence during treatment (41% success rate). These results suggest that this type of therapeutic community treatment may be unsuitable for those who cannot express their aggression in any other way than to themselves, and so, selection of such patients should be carefully monitored.

## CONCLUSIONS

To summarise from the previous (Rapoport, 1960; Whiteley, 1970; Copas and Whiteley, 1976; Norris, 1983; Gudjonsson and Roberts, 1982) and present studies of therapeutic community treatment at Henderson Hospital, the individual likely to succeed will be emotionally expressive, anxious, intropunitive and hostile, but not extremely aggressive nor markedly self-damaging, able to relate and with some degree of ego development. He or she will be an offender but not a recidivist, likely to have had psychiatric treatment and able to persist with the treatment for 6 months or more, gaining in self-esteem and becoming more independent and aspiring to less rule-breaking behaviour.

Psychological type has a bearing on future behaviour. The extra punitive personality who also has a high level of anxiety has the poorest prognosis for change with or without the therapeutic community model of treatment utilised here.

---

# REFERENCES

CAINE, T.M., FOULDS, G.A. & HOPE, K (1967) *Manual of Hostility and Direction of Hostility Questionnaire* Univ. London Press, London.

CLARKE, R.V.G. & CORNISH, D.B. (1972) *The controlled trial in institutional research.* HMSO, London.

CLECKLEY, H. (1964) *The Mask of Sanity* Mosby, St. Louis., Mo.

COPAS, J.B. (1983) Plotting p against x. *Applied Statistics* 32, pp 25-31.

COPAS, J.B. & WHITELEY, J.S. (1976) Predicting success in the treatment of psychopaths. *British Journal of Psychiatry* 129, pp 388-392.

ENDLER, N.S., HUNT, J. McV. & ROSENSTEIN, A.H. (1962) An S-R inventory of anxiousness. *Psychological Monographs* 76, No. 17

EVERITT, B.S. (1977) *The analysis of contingency tables.* Chapman & Hall, London.

EYSENCK, H. (1970) *Crime and Personality,* Paladin, London.

EYSENCK, H. & EYSENCK, S.B.G. (1964) *Manual of the Eysenck Personality Inventory,* Tavistock, London.

FOULDS, G.A. (1965) *Personality and personal illness.* Tavistock, London.

FOULDS, G.A., CAINE, T.M. & CREASY, M.A. (1960) Aspects of extra and intro-punitive expression in mental illness. *Journal of Mental Science,* 106, 599-610.

GUDJONSSON, G. & ROBERTS, J.C. (1982) Guilt and secondary self-concept in psychopaths. *Personality and Individual Differences.* 4, pp 65-70.

HARE, R.D. (1970) *Psychopathy: theory and research.* Wiley, New York.

HOPE, K. (1963) *The structure of hostility amongst normal and neurotic persons.* Ph.D. Thesis, University of London.

KARPMANN, B. (1947) Passive parasitic psychopathy: toward the personality structure and psychopathology of idiopathic psychopathy (antopathy) . *Psychoanalytic Review.* 34, pp 102-118; pp 198-222.

MANNING, N. (1979) Evaluating the therapeutic community. *Therapeutic Communities: reflections and progress.* Hinshelwood and Manning (eds.) RKP, London.

MARKS, I. (1965) Patterns of meaning in psychiatric patients. *Maudsley Monograph* Oxford Community Press, London.

NORRIS, M (1983) Changes in patients during treatment at the Henderson Hospital Therapeutic Community during 1977-1981. *British Journal of Medical Psychology* 56, pp 135-143.

O'BRIEN, M. (1976) *Psychopathic disorder.* Ph.D. Thesis, University of London.

RAPOPORT, R. (1960) *Community as doctor.* London: Tavistock Publishers.

RASMUSSEN, J.E. (1964) Relationship of ego identity to psychosocial effectiveness. *Psychological Reports* 15, pp 815-825.

ROBINS, L.N. (1966) *Deviant children grown up.* Williams & Wilkins, Baltimore, Md.

WHITELEY, J.S. (1970) The response of psychopaths to a therapeutic community. *British Journal of Psychiatry*, 116, pp 534-529

WHITELEY, J.S., BRIGGS, D. & TURNER, M (1972) *Dealing with deviants.* Hogarth Press, London

# Therapeutic Community Treatment for Personality Disordered Adults:
## Changes in Neurotic Symptomatology on Follow-up

Bridget Dolan, Chris Evans & James Wilson.

*International Journal of Social Psychiatry*
*1992, Vol. 38: pp 243-250*

Personality disordered patients are important as they place high continuing demands on services and are often refractory to traditional treatments. Often personality disorders may co-exist with neurotic symptomatology, worsening prognosis of the latter. This paper reports change in neurotic symptomatology following intensive, long term, therapeutic community treatment for such patients. Sixty two subjects with personality disorder were followed up for eight months after discharge (response rate 65%). Results showed a highly significant reduction in symptomatic distress as measured by the SCL-90R questionnaire. Investigation of the reliability and clinical importance of the change in individual subjects demonstrated that 55% of subjects had improved reliably, and in 32% this change was also clinically significant, whilst only 6.5% of subjects had deteriorated.

## INTRODUCTION

Personality disorder makes up substantial morbidity both in psychiatric populations and in the general community (Casey and Tyrer, 1990; Reich et al., 1989). The refractory nature of personality problems creates immense service load and nihilistic responses (Perry et al., 1987; Lewis & Appleby, 1988). Severely personality disordered patients tend to present in crises necessitating admission which is followed by rapid discharge (often unplanned) once each crisis has passed (Perry and Klerman, 1980) or they consume large amounts of staff time and emotion in Accident and Emergency departments through intrapunitive or extrapunitive impulsivity. These enacted problems 'suck in' services in a reactive and unconstructive manner and can distract from affective distress (Tyrer and Seivewright, 1988).

A major problem in the management of personality disordered individuals is that the 'personality' problems may co-exist with linked, secondary or coincidental 'symptom' disorders (Fyer et al., 1988) markedly worsening the prognosis of the latter. This impaired prognosis may result from failure to detect or accurately diagnose the personality disorder. Alternatively, if the personality disorder is detected, it may lead to therapeutic pessimism and subsequent inadequate assessment or treatment of the symptom disorder (Thompson and Goldberg, 1987). Waldinger (1987) has reviewed psychodynamic approaches to treatment noting the therapeutic difficulties which are such that Kernberg (1982) has recommended long term therapeutic community admission as the treatment of choice for patients who could not sustain outpatient psychotherapy.

## THE TREATMENT PROGRAMME AND CLIENTELE

The setting of the present study, Henderson Hospital, offers a therapeutic community treatment for personality disordered patients (Whiteley, 1980). The term 'therapeutic community' was coined in the 1940's (Main, 1946). It denotes a change away from an authoritarian system toward more active participation of patients in their own treatment and a collaborative style of staff behaviour. The traditional "medical model" which puts the patient in a passive position is avoided. All social interactions whether staff-staff, staff-patient or patient-patient can be closely examined and commented upon by all. In this process deviant behaviour can be picked up and understood. Henderson Hospital offers therapeutic community treatment for young adults (17-45 years) suffering from marked disturbance of emotional and/or social functioning (i.e. personality disorders of marked to severe degree).

Active participation is central: community members are called "residents" not patients, no psychotropic medicine is used, nor are any residents admitted under Probation Orders with a condition of treatment or any section of the Mental Health Act. Therapy takes place informally via the social milieu and in groups: daily community meeting, small group psychotherapy, activity groups, psychodrama and art therapy. There is no individual therapy, the aspiration is that the 'doctor' is the community itself (Jones, 1952; Rapoport, 1960).

Half of all referrals have a forensic history, 55% are from psychiatrists, and the majority have had previous psychiatric treatment. A recent investigation (Dolan, 1991) showed that 87% of residents met DSM-IIIR criteria for borderline personality disorder and that 95% met criteria for at least one cluster B axis 2 diagnosis. However, formal psychiatric diagnosis beyond 'personality disorder' is rarely referred to within Henderson. 'Symptoms' are not the focus of therapy, instead the community concentrates upon the meaning of individuals' feelings or actions, and on their relationships with others (residents and staff). More detailed descriptions of the treatment programme and clients have been published (e.g. Whiteley, 1980; Dolan and Norton, 1990).

An early investigation of outcome (Whiteley, 1970) considered 112 consecutively admitted male residents between one and three years after discharge. Of those with previous convictions 38% remained free of conviction, the same percentage of those with previous hospitalisation remained out of hospital. Subsequent studies of factors predictive of recidivism and re-admission found that the effect of age, gender and martial status was negligible, and that criminal and psychiatric history were poor prognostic factors (Copas and Whiteley, 1976). Copas, O'Brien, Roberts and Whiteley (1984), showed that success rate improved with length of stay, from 32% for those admitted for three months or less to 71% for those who stay over nine months. The success rate was lowest for the group showing high anxiety and extrapunitiveness.

To complement earlier reports of behaviour change following therapy at Henderson Hospital, the present report considers changes in symptomatic distress from pre-admission to eight month follow-up.

## METHODS

*Subjects*: All residents admitted after January 1985 and discharged by December 1988 were included in the study. This gave a total of 95 subjects. Ages ranged from 17 to 44 years with a mean of 25 years (s.d. 6.2; 95% C.I. 23.8 to 26.2)

*Instrument:* The SCL-90R is a self report questionnaire which measures symptomatic psychological distress, (Derogatis, Rickels and Rock, 1976). The 90 items are scored on a five point Likert scale from 0-4 and a General

Severity Index (GSI) is calculated from the average item scores. The SCL-90R has been shown to be valid and reliable measure (Derogatis, 1983) and has been applied in a variety of psychotherapeutic studies as both a screening tool and an outcome measure (Horowitz, Krupnik, Kaltreder & Alvarez, 1981; Blaszczynski & McConaghy, 1988). However, although the original authors suggest nine symptomatic subscales, current work suggests that nine factors do not hold up to analysis and that the scale is best used as a single-factor measure (e.g.: Hoffman and Overall, 1978; Holcomb, Adams and Ponder, 1983; Cyr, McKenna-Foley and Peacock, 1985).

*Procedure:* All people who were assessed for admission during the study period were asked to complete the SCL-90R before assessment. Subjects were posted the questionnaire with a letter explaining that the questionnaire was part of a research study, that participation was completely voluntary and that response would in no way affect their selection for treatment. (Further details of the selection process and a comparison of SCL profiles of people admitted with those assessed but not accepted are outlined in: Dolan, Morton & Wilson, 1990). Those subjects admitted (N=95) were asked to complete the SCL-90R again six months after discharge. The post discharge questionnaire was mailed to subjects six months after leaving Henderson at the discharge address provided. If no response was received up to three further mailings were used.

*Analyses:* The internal reliability of the SCL-90R in this sample was checked by calculating coefficient alpha using data from all 95 subjects from the pre-admission questionnaire (Cronbach, 1951). An alpha value of .97 was found indicating high internal reliability. Group mean change from admission to follow-up was tested for statistical significance using p=0.05 and paired t-tests and 95% confidence intervals (CI) of group means were calculated (Gardner and Altman, 1990).

Length of stay was analysed as a continuous variable and, to facilitate comparison with Copas et al., (1984), after trichotomising as: up to three months, three to nine months, over nine months.

Individual changes were examined for reliability and clinical significance of the change using the methods of Jacobson & Truax (1991). *Reliable change* (RC) is that which exceeds 1.96 × the standard error of measurement which would be expected in only 5% of subjects if change is due to unreliability of measurement alone. RC was derived using from the observed s.d. of initial scores of .73 and their alpha reliability coefficient as suggested by Jacobson, Follette & Revenstorf (1984). (The alpha coefficient of internal reliability was .97 for the initial data on all 95 subjects and .92 in those with complete data). The criterion value is: $1.96 \times 1.414 \times 0.73 \times (1-.92)^{.5}$ = 0.57). To show *clinically significant change* (SC) the subject must have an admission score making it more likely s/he is a member of the admission patient sample and a follow-up score more likely to belong to that of the normal population. This was determined applying Jacobson and Truax (1991) method $c$ to GSI scores t-score transformed with reference to non-patient normative data for the appropriate gender (Derogatis, 1983) giving a sample mean of 75.2 (s.d. 7.8) and reference mean of 50 (s.d. 10) hence an "equiprobable" criterion of 64.

## RESULTS

Ninety-five subjects completed the pre-admission SCL-90R, of these 62 (65%) completed the post-discharge questionnaire and a further 17 (17.9%) were returned undelivered. No contact or reply was obtained from 10 (10.5%) subjects whilst only 6 (6.3%) subjects refused to answer the questionnaire. The final group consisted of 33 women and 29 men. Their average length of stay on the unit was 30 weeks with a range from 4 to 55 weeks. The mean length of time between discharge and completion of the follow-up questionnaire was 8.2 months.

The mean pre-admission scores of the 62 subjects who completed the follow-up questionnaire (mean 1.83; s.d. 0.74; 95% CI 1.6 to 2.0) were compared with those of the 33 subjects who did not (mean 1.76; s.d. .84; 95% CI 1.5 to 2.1). There was no significant difference between the groups.

Comparison of pre-admission and follow-up scores showed a significant reduction in the Global Symptom Index after discharge (Follow-up: mean 1.13; s.d. 0.84, CI 0.9-1.3; t=6.1; P=<.0005). This indicates an overall reduction in the distress caused by symptoms.

Length of stay for the 95 residents ranged from 4 to 57 weeks (mean 28, S.D. 18.2, 95% C.I. 24 to 35 weeks). In total 30 (32%) of the residents stayed less than three months "short stay"; 30 (32%) stayed between six and nine months "medium stay" and 35 (36%) stayed longer than nine months "long stay".

When stay was analysed as a continuous variable, length of stay was not significantly related to improvement, nor did analysis of variance by stay groups reveal any statistically significant difference. However, residents in the long stay group tended to show greater improvement than both the short and medium stay group (mean improvement of .73 (s.d. .84) for the longer stay; vs. .58 (.86) for the medium stay and .61 (1.1) for the short stay group).

**Table 1**

**SCL-90R Global Symptom Index**
**Reliable and clinically significant change of individual subjects**

| Admission to follow-up | Reliable deterioration | Change not reliable | Reliable improvement | Total (%) |
|---|---|---|---|---|
| Normal - patient | 1 | 2 | - | 3 (5%) |
| Normal - normal | - | 2 | - | 2 (3%) |
| Patient - patient | 3 | 20 | 14 | 37 (60%) |
| Patient - normal | - | - | 20 | 20 (32%) |
| TOTAL | 4 | 24 | 34 | |
| **Total %** | **6.5%** | **38.5%** | **55.0%** | 100% |

Table 1 presents individual change calculations which showed that 34 (55%) had a reliable improvement in total GSI score. Of these, 20 (32% of the total) showed clinically significant improvement whilst 14 (23%) did not, i.e. had improved but were still not in the "normal range". Two subjects (3%) whose admission scores placed them in the "normal range" remained there on follow-up and did not show reliable change in either direction. Twenty subjects (32%) remained in the "patient range" and also showed no reliable change in either direction. Three subjects (4.5%) who began in the "normal range" moved into the "patient range" but the size of the change was reliable in only one. Three subjects (5%) showed a reliable deterioration in SCL score remaining in the "patient range".

## DISCUSSION

These results show that the subjects had high scores for general symptomatology on admission, and that there were marked improvements in symptomatology in subjects completing the follow-up questionnaire.

Several methodological concerns affect interpretation of the data. The 65% response rate for the study was good for such a client group not in continuing treatment by the unit given the low response rates to other mailed surveys of personality disordered subjects (e.g. Robertson and Gunn, 1987). Eighteen per cent of the loss to follow-up was attributable to the mobility of this population. Those who responded on follow-up had similar admission GSI scores to those who did not, and the variance of the admission scores did not differ markedly from that of the follow-up scores nor were the variances of the admission scores of the responders markedly different from those of the non-responders.

Given these caveats it remains of interest that the mean admission scores exceeded those reported by Derogatis (1983) for a sample of 313 psychiatric inpatients (mean 1.30; s.d. 0.82) and the GSI scores closely matched those reported by Vaglum et al., (1990) for a sample of therapeutic community day patients with severe personality disorders (mean 1.87, s.d. 0.6). This finding of high rates of neurotic symptomatology links with other work (e.g. Gunn & Robertson, 1976; Copas et al., 1984) demonstrating that personality disordered patients who have accepted some form of treatment, do not fit the stereotype of the "affectless state" of psychopathy but express considerable neurotic upset. The presence of this neurotic pathology is particularly important in the light of the evidence that personality disordered patients with co-existing neurotic symptomatology do worse in treatment than those without (Fyer et al., 1988).

In line with the findings of Copas et al., (1984) we found a tendency for improvement on follow-up to be related to longer stay. However, the relationship between length of stay and neurotic symptomatic improvement investigated in this study was perhaps less strong than might have been expected. The association was confined only to tendencies for the group who stayed longer to improve more on the total SCL-90R score. This could be naively taken as an indication that a shorter term of therapy is sufficient for determining therapeutic change. However it must be remembered that the present study only considers one aspect of outcome, neurotic symptomatology. In this group of personality disordered people a wide range of behavioural, emotional and personality problems are evident but the amelioration of these other aspects after therapy was not considered. Clearly, improvement following therapy will be related to a wide range of variables (including pre-morbid state; demographic and clinical features; events during therapy; therapists' characteristics etc.) therefore it would be presumptuous to expect a strong linear relationship to a single variable such as time in therapy. Certainly Copas et al., (1984) found that those residents who stayed longer at Henderson were less likely to have re-admission to psychiatric hospital or re-conviction in the following three years. We would suggest that it is important to take a wider view both of improvement and of factors contributing to it.

Nevertheless, the results clearly show a significant decrease in distress caused by symptoms following treatment at Henderson Hospital. The change shown in this study is not only a statistically significant overall change but, perhaps a more clinically digestible finding, over half the subjects showed reliable improvement and in one third this change was also clinically significant and only 6.5% showed reliable deterioration. This is important in the light of the therapeutic nihilism held by psychiatrists when considering the management of these patients (Lewis and Appleby, 1988). Even if all the non-responders were more likely to have been those who had deteriorated, it would still remain that at least one third of the 95 admissions showed improvements in neurotic symptomatology.

The design of the study did not include a control population, thus we can not be sure that the improvement found in this sample could not also be found in less intense treatment or even with no treatment at all. However, the policy not to admit patients in acute crisis makes it unlikely that the findings are a result of regression to the mean. Additionally, we were not able to take account of a range of possible life events (including having further therapy) which may have occurred between discharge and completion of the follow-up questionnaire.

Further studies are in progress to ascertain how improvement in neurotic symptoms is related to the residents characterological disorder, demographic features and the course of treatment.

# REFERENCES

BLASZCZYNSKI, A.P., MCCONAGHY, N. (1988) SCL-90 assessed psychopathology in pathological gamblers. *Psychological Reports* 62 (2), pp 547-52.

CASEY, P.R., TYRER, P. (1990) Personality disorder and psychiatric illness in general practice. *British Journal of Psychiatry* 156; pp 261-265.

COPAS, J.B., WHITELEY, S. (1976) Predicting success in the treatment of psychopaths. *British Journal of Psychiatry* 129; pp 388-392

COPAS, J.B., O'BRIEN, M., ROBERTS, J., WHITELEY, S. (1984) Treatment outcome in personality disorder: The effect of social, psychological and behavioural variables. *Personality and Individual Differences* Vol. 5(5) pp 565-573.

CRONBACH, L.J. (1951) Coefficient alpha and the internal structure of tests. *Psychometrika.* 16,(3); pp 297-334.

CYR, J.J., MCKENNA-FOLEY, J.M. & PEACOCK, E. (1985) Factor structure of the SCL-90: is there one? *Journal of Personality Assessment* 49 (6), pp 571-578.

DEROGATIS, L.R. (1983) *SCL-90R, Administration, Scoring and Procedures Manual.* Second edition. Clinical Psychometric Research, New York.

DEROGATIS, L.R., RICKELS, K., ROCK, A. (1976) SCL-90 and the MMPI a step in the validation of a new self-report scale. *British Journal of Psychiatry* 128, pp 280-289

DOLAN, B.M. (1991) Gender issues in impulsive behaviour. Conference paper presented at *"Perspectives on Women and Violence"*, London.

DOLAN, B.M., MORTON, A., WILSON, J. (1990) Acceptance by the Henderson selection group: Association with degree and type of psychological distress. *International Journal of Social Psychiatry* 36(4), pp 265-271.

DOLAN, B.M., NORTON, K. (1990) Is there a need for specialist psychiatric units in the NHS ? Henderson Hospital: A case in point. *Psychiatric Bulletin* 14; pp 72-76.

FYER, M.R., FRANCIS, A.J, SULLIVAN, T.S., HURT, S.W., CLARKIN, J. (1988) Co-morbidity of borderline personality disorder. *Archives of General Psychiatry* 45; pp 348-352.

GARDNER, M.J., & ALTMAN, D.G. (1990) Confidence and clinical importance in research findings. *British Journal of Psychiatry* 156; pp 472-474.

GUNN, J. & ROBERTSON, G. (1976) Psychopathic personality: a conceptual problem. *Psychological Medicine* 6, pp 631-634.

HOFFMAN, N.G., OVERALL, P.B. (1978) Factor structure of the SCL-90 in a psychiatric population. *Journal of Consulting and Clinical Psychology* 46; pp 1187-1191

HOLCOMB, W.R., ADAMS, N.A., PONDER, H.M. (1983) Factor structure of the SCL-90 with acute psychiatric in-patients. *Journal of Consulting and Clinical Psychology* 51; pp 535-538.

HOROWITZ, M.J., KRUPNIK, J., KALTREIDER, N., ALVAREZ, W. (1981) Initial psychological response to parental death. *Archives of General Psychiatry* 38: pp 85-92.

JACOBSON, N.S., FOLLETTE, W.C., REVENSTORF, D. (1984) Psychotherapy outcome research: methods for reporting variability and evaluating clinical significance. *Behavior Therapy* 15, pp 336-352.

JACOBSON, N.S., REVENSTORF, D. (1988) Statistics for assessing the clinical significance of psychotherapy techniques: issues, problems, and new developments. *Behavioral Assessment* 10, pp 133-145

JACOBSON, N.S. & TRUAX, P. (1991) Clinical significance: a statistical approach to defining meaningful change in psychotherapy research. *Journal of Consulting and Clinical Psychology* 59(1), pp 12-19.

JONES, M. (1952) *Social psychiatry: a study of therapeutic communities* London: Tavistock.

KERNBERG, O. (1982) Advantages and liabilities of the therapeutic community. Pines M. (Ed) *The individual and the group* New York, Plenum Press.

LEWIS, G. & APPLEBY, L. (1988) Personality Disorder: The patients psychiatrists dislike. *British Journal of Psychiatry* 153, pp 44-49.

MAIN, T. (1946) The hospital as a therapeutic institution. *Bulletin of Menninger Clinic* Vol. 10; 3, pp 66-70

PERRY, J.C. & KLERMAN, G.L. (1980) Clinical features of borderline personality disorder. *American Journal of Psychiatry* 142, pp 15-21.

PERRY, J.C., LAVORI, P.W., HOKE, L. (1987) A Markove model for predicting levels of psychiatric service usage in borderline and anti-social personality disorders and bipolar type II affective disorder. *Journal of Psychiatric Research* 21(3) pp 215-232.

RAPOPORT, R (1960) *Community as Doctor.* Tavistock, London.

REICH, J., YATES, W. & NDUAGABA, M. (1989) Prevalence of DSM-III personality disorders in the community. *Social Psychiatry and Psychiatric Epidemiology* 24; pp 12-16.

ROBERTSON, G. & GUNN, J. (1987) A ten-year follow-up of men discharged from Grendon Prison. *British Journal of Psychiatry* 151, pp 674-678.

THOMPSON, D.J. & GOLDBERG, D. (1987) Hysterical personality disorder: the process of diagnosis in clinical and experimental settings. *British Journal of Psychiatry* 150, pp 241-245.

TYRER, P. & SEIVEWRIGHT, H. (1988) Studies of outcome. In: *Personality disorders: Diagnosis, management and course* (1988) Tyrer P.(Ed) Wright, London.

VAGLUM, P. et al. (1990) Treatment response of severe and non-severe personality disorders in a therapeutic community day unit. *Journal of Personality Disorders* 4(2) pp 161-172.

WALDINGER, R.J. (1987) Intensive psychodynamic therapy with borderline patients: An overview. *American Journal of Psychiatry* 144: 3; pp 267-274.

WHITELEY, J.S. (1970) The response of psychopaths to a therapeutic community. *British Journal of Psychiatry* 116; pp 517-529

WHITELEY, J.S. (1980) The Henderson Hospital. *International Journal of Therapeutic Communities* 1(1); pp 38-57.

# Change in Borderline Symptoms One Year after Therapeutic Community Treatment for Severe Personality Disorder

Bridget Dolan, Fiona Warren and Kingsley Norton

*British Journal of Psychiatry*
*(1997) 171, pp 274-279*

The view that severe personality disorder (SPD) is untreatable derives from poor-quality studies of treatment outcome which use indirect measures of SPD pathology. This study evaluates the impact of psychotherapeutic in-patient treatment on core personality disorder symptoms. 137 SPD patients completed the Borderline Syndrome Index (BSI) on referral and one year post-treatment ('admitted' n=70) or one year post-referral ('non-admitted', n=67); 22 of the non-admitted group were refused extra-contractual referral funding for their treatment. There was a significantly greater reduction in BSI scores in the treated than in the non-admitted group. Changes in BSI scores were significantly positively correlated with length of treatment. Assessment of the reliability and clinical significance of changes in individual subjects showed that the magnitude of this change was reliable and clinically significant in 42.9% of the admitted sample, compared with only 17.9% of the non-admitted sample (18.2% of the unfunded group). Specialist in-patient treatment is effective in reducing core SPD psychopathology.

## INTRODUCTION

In spite of increasing interest in severe personality disorder (SPD), it is clear from recent government reports and literature reviews that knowledge of effective treatments for SPD is rudimentary (Dolan & Coid, 1993; Reed, 1994). Although SPD patients are notoriously difficult to engage in research studies, part of the lack of evidence of treatment efficacy stems from the researchers themselves, not simply from their subjects. The design of most outcome studies is inadequate, hence they yield little convincing evidence that personality disorder either can or cannot be treated effectively (Dolan & Coid, 1993). One result is a prevailing mood of therapeutic pessimism, rather than healthy scepticism, about the treatability of personality disorder.

The accurate assessment of change in SPD is hampered by the use of only indirect measures of the core psychopathology and by the failure to link outcome measures to the treatment focus. Many outcome studies fail to assess the impact of treatment on aspects intrinsic to the personality disorder pathology itself, separately form those which are only associated or indirect phenomena. Indeed, there is a range of features associated with personality disorder, changes in which are erroneously equated with change in the personality disorder itself, such as reduction in axis 1 diagnosis symptomatology, or behavioural features such as criminal activity, self-mutilation or suicidality. Other common methodological imperfections include small sample sizes and uncontrolled study designs with short post-treatment follow-up (see Norton & Dolan, 1995, for a review of these issues). It is appropriate to evaluate those parameters associated with SPD which are considered desirable outcomes in personality disordered patients, and understandable that research will favour the most easily measurable aspects. Total reliance upon such proxy measures of change may reflect the fact that instruments for measuring the phenomenology of personality disorders (whether based upon DSM-III-R/IV or ICD-10 classifications) are often ill equipped to assess change. Personality disorders are "long term patterns of functioning" (American Psychiatric Association, 1994) so it is difficult to demonstrate change with a short follow-up period. Indeed, on some core-defining criteria change is impossible (for example, evidence of a conduct disorder before age 15 for DSM-IV antisocial personality disorder). Measures of personality organisation such as Kernberg's (1981) structural interview for borderline personality organisation and the Personality Functioning Scale (Lingiardi *et al,* 1994) may have advantages in this respect over descriptive diagnostic methods.

This study aims to assess changes in core personality-disorder features one year after treatment in a group of patients with SPD referred for specialist in-patient psychotherapy in a democratic therapeutic community. Comparison is made between those admitted and those not admitted for treatment. One-third of the subjects were not admitted because funding for their treatment was refused by their local purchasing authority; this subgroup form a superior comparison sample.

## METHOD

*Setting*
The study was conducted at Henderson Hospital, a national specialist (tertiary level) in-patient unit for SPD which employs a democratic therapeutic community approach (Jones, 1952). Therapy within the unit occurs in the formal daily programme of group meetings and more informally through sociotherapy deriving form the social milieu. The term 'therapeutic community' denotes a move away from an authoritarian to a more collaborative style of staff behaviour, including more active participation of patients in their own treatment and that of their peers. Responsibility for the day-to-day running of the therapeutic community is shared among patients and staff. This collaborative and democratic style, whereby the community itself is invested with an important decision-making function, forms a cornerstone of therapy (Norton, 1992). The unit has 29 beds and male and female residents can stay for a maximum of one year. Treatment is voluntary, no psychotropic medication is used and all treatment is in a group setting. The clinical approach and therapy programme are described in greater detail elsewhere (Rapoport, 1960; Dolan, 1996).

*Procedure*
Consecutive referrals were mailed a self-report questionnaire pack on referral. A second follow-up pack was sent one year after referral to those who were not admitted, or one year after discharge to those who were. Up to three repeated mailings were used, to maximise response rate.

*Participants **and response rates***
The sample group consisted of all referrals to the hospital between September 1990 and November 1994. Of the 598 referrals, 380 (63.5%) returned completed baseline forms: 176 (77%) of the 228 admitted patients and 204 (55%) of the 370 non-admitted referrals. At one-year follow-up, 80 referrals could not be traced through their original address; 159 participants returned completed forms, representing 42% of the baseline sample of 380 (54.4% of the admitted and 53.2% of non-admitted group contacted) In total, 137 participants completed both a baseline and a follow-up questionnaire, and these formed the final study sample. Of these, 70 had been admitted for treatment and 67 were not admitted. Of the non-admitted sample, 18 (26.9%) were refused admission by the hospital on clinical

grounds, 27 (40.3%) did not attend assessment or admission appointments and 22 (32.8%) had funding of their treatment refused by their local District Health Authority. (Since creation of the internal market within the UK National Health Service in 1991, it has been necessary to have funding for tertiary-level treatments agreed by the patient's local District Health Authority. Such funding is not uncommonly refused for personality disordered patients (see Dolan et al, 1992) [1].

*Instruments*
*Borderline Syndrome Index (BSI)*
The BSI is a 52-item forced-choice measure designed to assess borderline psychopathology associated with both borderline personality disorder and borderline personality organisation (Conte *el al*, 1980). Scale items not only relate to psychiatric symptoms, but also concern interpersonal and interpersonal issues (e.g. "I am afraid to form close personal relationships"); some address impulsive and self-damaging aspects of borderline phenomena (e.g. "I want to hurt myself"; "I am bothered by murderous idea"); and others cover areas which are specifically addressed in therapeutic community treatment (e.g. "It scares me to take responsibility for anyone"; "I never feel as if I belong").

Good internal reliability of the BSI (alpha-coefficient 0.97) was found in an earlier study in the same unit (Dolan *et al,* 1992). Three-year test-retest reliability of 0.57 was reported by Fine & Sansone (1990), albeit from a small clinical sample. The BSI shows fair agreement with the clinical diagnosis of borderline personality disorder (DSM) (k=0.53, Conte *et al*, 1980; k=0.47, Lewis & Harder, 1991). Lower kappa values were reported against the PAS-derived borderline personality disorder category (Marlowe *et al*, 1996)

*Personality Diagnostic Questionnaire (PDQ-R)*
The PDQ-R (Hyler & Reider, 1987) is a 152-item self-report measure assessing the presence of criteria for the 11 subtypes of DSM-III-R personality disorder. The PDQ-R also contains and 'impairment distress'

---

[1] At the time of going to press, Henderson Hospital and its outreach service (HOST), and the two new therapeutic communities, Webb and Main Houses with their associated outreach services are centrally purchased. For the time being, therefore, the majority of referrals do not require negotiations about funding.

scale consisting of five items measuring disturbance in psychological, social and occupational functioning (in line with the GAF assessment of DSM-III-R). The PDQ-R has respectable test-retest reliability (mean k=0.58) and compares favourably with the interrater reliability for both clinical interview and semi-structured interview (Hurt et al, 1984). Median internal reliability of the personality disorder scales is reported as 0.69 (range 0.56-0.84).

*Analyses*

Pre-admission questionnaire data showed an alpha value of 0.92 for the BSI, indicating high internal reliability. To account for non-normal distribution, the statistical significance of group mean change from admission to follow-up was calculated with Mann-Whitney U-tests; 95% confidence intervals for the differences in means are also reported.

However, such group mean calculations provide no information about the effects of therapy for individual subjects. It is more important clinically to know whether individuals improve enough to resemble members of the general population, and the statistical 'significance' test imposes a criterion which may have little relevance to the clinician in this respect. An alternative method of analysing data allows evaluation of the clinical relevance of change in subjects with reference to a normal population (Jacobson *et al*, 1984). First, false positive scores must be excluded by looking at how reliable the change is. Reliable change is that which exceeds 1.96 x the standard error of measurement, which would be expected in only 5% of subjects if change is due to unreliability of measurement alone[2]. Even where change is reliable it may not mean that the patient is functioning as well as a non-patient. To demonstrate clinically significant change, the subject requires to have a pre-admission score which makes it more likely that she/he is a member of the admission patient sample and a follow-up score more likely to belong to that of the normal population[3].

Such methods of analysing data have previously been used to evaluate a range of therapies including dynamic psychotherapy (Aveline, 1995),

---

[2] 'Reliable change' was derived using the observed s.d. of initial scores of 9.98 and their $\alpha$ reliability coefficient. The criterion value is: $1.96 \times 1.414 \times 9.98 \times (1-092)^{05} = 7.82$.

[3] This was determined applying Jacobson & Truax' (1991) method c to BSI scores, with reference to non-patient normative data (provided by the BSI questionnaire's originators), giving sample mean of 34.08 (s.d 9.98) and reference mean of 5.92 (s.d. 5.5); hence an 'equiprobable' clinical significance criterion of 20.01

exposure-based intervention for agoraphobia (Jacobson *et al*, 1988) and behavioural marital therapy (Jacobson & Follette, 1985).

## RESULTS

*Personality disorder psychopathology*
In line with previous studies of this group of clients, subjects showed substantial personality disorder pathology as measured by the PDQ-R (Dolan et al, 1995). On average, subjects met or exceeded PDQ-R cut-off points for seven of the 11 DSM-III-R personality disorder categories, with borderline and paranoid personality disorder being most prevalent (both 80%). There was no difference between admitted and non-admitted samples in terms of prevalence of individual diagnoses, overall number of 'diagnoses', or level of impairment and distress, as measured by The PDQ-R (see Table 1).

*Relationship of BSI score to personality disorder diagnoses*
The presence of multiple personality disorder subtype diagnoses made testing the association of BSI scores with individual personality disorder subtypes impractical. Only three subjects scored in a single personality disorder subtype, and eight met criteria for all 11 PDQ-R categories. There was, however, a significant and positive correlation between the baseline total BSI score and the total number of individual PDQ categories per subject ($r=0.38$, $p<0.001$).

*Mean changes in BSI score*
There was no significant difference between the mean baseline BSI scores of the admitted and non-admitted groups. At follow-up, all groups showed some decrease in average symptom scores over time (see Table 2). However, a Mann-Whitney *U-test* reveled a significantly greater reduction in symptoms in the admitted sample than in the non-admitted groups ($p<0.0013$).

**Table I  PDQ-R diagnoses of personality disorder**

| Personality disorder category | Admitted sample, % (n=70) | Non-admitted sample, % (n=67) | 95% CI difference (admitted v. non-admitted) | Unfunded sample, % (n=22) | 95% CI difference (admitted v. unfunded) |
|---|---|---|---|---|---|
| **Schizoid** | 57 | 70 | -0.29 to 0.03 | 55 | -0.21 to 0.26 |
| **Schizotpal** | 57 | 69 | -0.27 to 0.04 | 64 | -0.29 to 0.17 |
| **Paranoid** | 83 | 76 | -0.07 to 0.20 | 64 | -0.03 to 0.40 |
| **Avoidant** | 67 | 58 | -0.07 to 0.25 | 45 | -0.02 to 0.45 |
| **Dependent** | 74 | 69 | -0.10 to 0.20 | 59 | -0.08 to 0.35 |
| **Obsessive-compulsive** | 61 | 66 | -0.20 to 0.12 | 68 | -0.30 to 0.16 |
| **Passive-aggressive** | 70 | 64 | -0.10 to 0.22 | 64 | -0.16 to 0.29 |
| **Histrionic** | 59 | 69 | -0.26 to 0.06 | 73 | -0.40 to 0.02 |
| **Narcissistic** | 58 | 52 | -0.10 to 0.23 | 64 | -0.28 to 0.18 |
| **Borderline** | 80 | 81 | -0.14 to 0.13 | 68 | -0.09 to 0.37 |
| **Antisocial** | 52 | 51 | -0.16 to 0.17 | 55 | -0.27 to 0.21 |
| **Total PDQ categories mean (s.d.)** | 7.15 (2.6) | 7.23 (2.4) | -0.85 to 0.70 | 6.8 (2.8) | -0.94 to 1.6 |
| **Impairment & distress mean (s.d.)** | 3.97 (1.2) | 4.2 (1.0) | -0.6 to 0.14 | 4.36 (0.95) | -0.95 to 1.7 |

**Table 2. Mean (s.d) Borderline Syndrome Index scores at referral and one-year follow-up**

| | Referral | Follow-up | Mean change | 95% CI difference from treated sample | Mann-Whitney *U*-test of difference (*P* value) |
|---|---|---|---|---|---|
| **Admitted (n=70)** | 34.6 (9.4) | 20.3 (14.8) | 14.3 (13.7) | - | - |
| **Non-admitted (n=67)** | 33.3 (10.6) | 26.9 (13.4) | 6.4 (12.2) | 3.5 to 12.3 | 0.0013 |
| *Non-admitted subgroups* | | | | | |
| Non funded (n=22) | 33.5 (11.6) | 28.4 (14.9) | 5.1 (10.6) | 2.9 to 15.5 | 0.004 |
| **Did not attend/ cancelled (n=27)** | 30.5 (11.2) | 24.3 (13.6) | 6.14 (13.1) | 2.1 to 14.2 | 0.016 |
| **Not selected (n=18)** | 37.6 (6.6) | 29.3 (10.9) | 8.3 (12.7) | -1.1 to 13.1 | NS |

### Reliability and clinical significance of changes

The analysis of the reliability and clinical significance of the changes in individual subjects (as described above) showed that 61% of the admitted group had improved reliably, compared with 37% of the total non-admitted group and 23% of the unfunded group (see Table 3). The magnitude of this change was also clinically significant in 43% of the admitted sample, compared with only 18% of the non-admitted sample and 18% of the un-funded group.

This difference in proportions was significant, at $P=0.0015$ (admitted v. non-admitted) and $P=0.036$ (admitted v. non-funded). In addition, 6% of the non-admitted sample were now functioning at a reliably worse level, compared with only 3% of the admitted group, although this difference in proportions was not significant.

### Relationship of outcome to length of stay in treatment

The admitted group stayed for an average of seven months (range 1-52 weeks). The change in BSI score was found to be significantly positively correlated with length of stay in treatment ($r=0.42$; $P<0.001$). There was also a significant difference between the length of stay of the 30 admitted patients who showed clinically significant change and those who did not (mean 35.7 weeks (s.d 2.7) v. 2.1 weeks (s.d. 3.2) (Mann-Whitney $U$-test $P=0.0006$).

### DISCUSSION

This study demonstrates considerable changes in personality disorder psychopathology one year after discharge from specialist in-patient therapeutic community treatment. This reduction was significantly greater for the treated sample than for a non-admitted group of referrals. However, the treatment goal of specialist in-patient psychotherapy (and the wishes of most referrers and patients) is not simply to show an overall group average function in scale scores on a measure (as shown in statistical significance tests), but for the patient to return to normal functioning. Evaluation of the

## Table 3. Change in individuals' BSI scores

| | Reliable improvement % | Clinically significant change, % | Both reliable & clinical change, % | 95% CI difference in proportions from admitted sample | $\chi^2$ P value |
|---|---|---|---|---|---|
| **Admitted (n=70)** | 61.4 | 42.9 | 42.9 | - | - |
| **Non-admitted (n=67)** | 37.3 | 22.4 | 17.9 | 0.1 to 0.4 | 0.0015 |
| ***Non-admitted subgroups*** | | | | | |
| **Non funded (n=22)** | 22.7 | 18.2 | 18.2 | 0.05 to 0.45 | 0.036 |
| **Did not attend/cancelled (n=27)** | 40.7 | 29.6 | 18.5 | 0.06 to 0.43 | 0.025 |
| **Not selected (n=18)** | 50.0 | 16.7 | 16.7 | 0.05 to 0.47 | 0.041 |

clinical relevance of the individual changes revealed that a greater proportion of the admitted than of the non-admitted group showed reliable and clinically significant improvements (43% admitted v. 8% non-admitted) which were positively related to length of stay in treatment.

The findings of this study complement earlier work from Henderson Hospital, which has shown that admission to this specialist therapeutic community significantly reduces rates of subsequent re-admission to hospital and re-conviction over a five-year follow-up period (Copas *et al*, 1984), resulting in considerable future cost-offset (Dolan et al, 1996). However, although positive psychological changes during therapeutic community treatment have been shown (Norris, 1983) no previous studies from the Unit have directly addressed outcome in terms of core personality disorder features, as opposed to psychological and behavioural manifestations of SPD.

*Non-funded comparison sample*
This is one of the first prospective studies of change in core features of personality disorder after in-patient treatment to include an adequate comparison sample. Although previously positive comparisons have been shown between those treated at Henderson Hospital and non-admitted subjects (Copas *et al,* 1984), or subjects admitted to other units (Norris, 1983), such comparisons do not represent adequate control samples since the factors leading to non-admission or admission elsewhere may also be pertinent to outcome. The unfunded sample in the current study thus presents a superior comparison group, although still not a matched control sample.

There are both practical and ethical difficulties in withholding a scarce treatment resource form patients in need of it, and this has previously precluded collection of randomly controlled research samples in our unit. However, the structural and procedural changes in the National Health Service since 1991 provided the opportunity to collect more adequate (although still imperfect) control/comparison samples. Refusal to grant funding for tertiary treatment in the unit has been shown to be made on financial rather than clinical grounds. Previously no differences were found in clinical and psychological features between those referrals whose funding was agreed and those whose funding was refused (Dolan *et al,* 1994). Such refusal of treatment funding, although clinically abhorrent, has proved advantageous to the research programme in generating a more representative comparison sample than previously deemed ethically possible.

It is therefore noteworthy that the unfunded subsample in the present study showed the smallest overall reduction in group mean score, and fewer of this group showed reliable improvements when compared with the admitted sample and the other two non-admitted groups ('non-selected' and 'cancelled' referrals).

*Length of stay*
As in previous studies from the Unit, length of stay in treatment was influential in that it was positively correlated with improvements in borderline psychopathology on follow-up. Those who showed clinically significant change had, on average, stayed nine months in therapy. Previous studies have shown a correlation between less use of services after discharge (at five-year follow-up) and increased length of stay (Copas *et al,* 1984).

*Methodological limitations*
The use of self-reporting has meant that the study has methodological limitations. The follow-up response rate is greater than might be expected in a postal survey of personality-disordered individuals, since the use of three mailings substantially enhanced the return rate. However, although the follow-up response rates for those whose addresses were known were similar for both the admitted and on-admitted samples (54.4 *v.* 53.2%), the extent to which the results can be generalised may be questioned. The follow-up interval differed between samples, since the non-admitted group were re-tested one year after referral while the admitted group were re-tested one year after their discharge from treatment. Although the non-admitted sample did show some improvements in their borderline symptoms, many non-admitted referrals will have received some non-specialist treatment in their local services in the intervening year which could not be controlled for.

The BSI, as used in this study, is a measure of change in a range of borderline personality characteristics, and does not equate to a clinical diagnosis of borderline personality disorder. However, the significant correlation of the BSI with initial severity of personality disorder (as measured by the PDQ-R) and the positive association of BSI change scores with length of stay in treatment provide some support for the sensitivity of the BSI as a measure of change.

It remains a possibility that the changes in BSI score identified in our sample are related to changes in axis I disorder, particularly given that patients may be referred for specialist treatment at a time of some life crisis when depression and anxiety are high. It is also to be expected that there would be some regression to the mean in both treated and non-admitted patient groups, given the likelihood that patients are referred to our tertiary-level service when particularly symptomatic. In a recent study (Remington & Book, 1993), high scores on the BSI were related to chronicity of dysthymia, but that research was based on a small sample of seven subjects with dysthymia alone and seven with borderline personality disorder alone; given the small sample size and very common comorbidity of the two conditions, that work needs replication. To elucidate this point further, data on changes in axis I symptoms alongside personality disorder changes are currently being collected at Henderson Hospital.

## CONCLUSIONS

This study demonstrates the efficacy of specialist in-patient psychotherapy in reducing borderline symptoms at one-year follow-up. Not only do patients improve in overall group mean scores, but also a substantial proportion make a clinically meaningful return to 'normal functioning'. We suggest that the therapeutic pessimism surrounding change in core personality disorder symptoms may be more a response to feelings of frustration and nihilism elicited by these patients in therapy than to empirical data. In fact, there are few empirical studies at all to support the idea that this group is 'untreatable'. When outcome measures are tailored to the actual focus of treatment, as in this study, the results are encouraging. We believe that with appropriate specialist treatment tailored to the specific needs of the patient group, significant and meaningful clinical improvements in severe personality disorder can be achieved. Given these findings, we consider it important to continue with research to determine what are the therapeutic ingredients of the 'package' offered at the Henderson Hospital, and the possibility of their application in order settings.

## CLINICAL IMPLICATIONS

- Core personality disorder psychopathology is treatable but careful consideration should be given to the type of treatment offered to this group of patients.
- Specialist therapeutic community treatment can effect clinically meaningful improvements in severe personality disorder.
- Refusing to fund specialist treatment of severe personality disorder deprives patients of an important opportunity for improvement.

## LIMITATIONS

- Many personality-disordered patients are unsuitable for therapeutic community treatment.
- The comparison sample of unfunded patients falls short of an experimental control group.
- The impact of axis I disorder on outcome was not assessed.

## ACKNOWLEDGEMENTS

*This study was supported by a grant from South Thames (West) Regional Health Authority Research and Development funds. We are, as ever, grateful to Dr Chris Evans for his helpful comments on the manuscript.*

## REFERENCES

AMERICAN PSYCHIATRIC ASSOCIATION (1994) *Diagnostic and Statistical Manual of Mental Disorders* (4th end) (DSM-IV). Washington, DC: APA

AVELINE, M. (1995) Assessing the value of brief intervention at the time of assessment for dynamic psychotherapy. In: *Research Foundations for Psychotherapy Practice* (eds M. Aveline & D. Shapiro), pp 129-150. Chichester: Wiley

CONTE, H. R., PLUTCHIK, R., KARASU, T. B., et al (1980) A self-report borderline scale: Discriminant validity and preliminary norms. *Journal of Nervous and Mental Disease,* 168, pp 428-435

COPAS, J. B., O'BRIEN, M., ROBERTS, J. C., et al (1984) Treatment outcome in personality disorder: The effect of social, psychological and behavioural variables. *Personality and Individual Differences,* 5, pp 565-573

DOLAN, B. (1996) *Perspectives on Henderson Hospital,* Sutton: Henderson Hospital

DOLAN, B. & COID, J. (1993) Psychopathic and Antisocial Personality Disorders: *Treatment and Research Issues,* London: Gaskell

DOLAN, B., EVANS, C & NORTON, K. (1992) The Separation Individuation Inventory: Association with borderline phenomena. *Journal of Nervous and Mental Disease,* 180, pp 529-533

DOLAN B.M., EVANS, C. & NORTON, K. (1994) Funding treatment of offender patients with severe personality disorder: Do financial considerations trump clinical need? *Journal of Forensic Psychiatry,* 5, pp 263-274

DOLAN, B.M., EVANS, C.D. & NORTON, K. (1995) Multiple Axis-II diagnosis of personality disorders. *British Journal of Psychiatry,* 166, pp 107-112

DOLAN, B.M., WARREN, F.M., MENZIES, D. & NORTON, K. (1996) Cost-offset following specialist treatment of severe personality disorders. *Psychiatric Bulletin,* 20, pp 413-417

FINE, M. A. & SANSONE, R. (1990) Three-year test-retest reliability of the Borderline Syndrome Index among women with eating disorders. *Psychological Reports,* 67, pp 1089-1090

HURT, S. W., HYLER, S.E., FRANCES, A., et al (1984) Assessing borderline personality disorder with self-report, clinical interview, or semi-structured interview. *American Journal of Psychiatry,* 141, pp 1228-1231

HYLER, S & REIDER, R. O. (1987) *Personality Diagnostic Questionnaire Revised (PDQ-R).* New York: New York State Psychiatric Institute

JACOBSON, N. S & FOLLETTE, W. C. (1985) Clinical significance of improvement resulting from two behavioral marital therapy components. *Behavior Therapy,* 16, pp 249-262

JACOBSON, N. S & TRUAX, P. (1991) Clinical significance: a statistical approach to defining meaningful change in psychotherapy research. *Journal of Consulting and Clinical Psychology,* 59, pp 12-19

JACOBSON, N. S FOLLETTE, W. C. & REVENSTORF, D (1984) Psychotherapy outcome research: Methods for reporting variability and evaluating clinical significance. *Behavior Therapy,* 15, 336-352

JACOBSON, N. S WILSON, L. & TUPPER, C (1988) The clinical significance of treatment gains resulting from exposure-based interventions for agoraphobia: A re-analysis of outcome data. *Behavior Therapy,* 19, pp 539-554

JONES, M. (1952) Social Psychiatry: *A Study of Therapeutic Communities.* London: Tavistock

KERNBERG, O (1981) Structural interviewing. *Psychiatric Clinics of North America,* 1, pp 169-195

LEWIS, S & HARDER, D. W (1991) A comparison of four measure to diagnose DSM-III-R Borderline Personality Disorder in outpatients. *Journal of Nervous and Mental Disease,* 179, pp 329-337.

LINGIARDI, V., MADEDDU, F., FOSSATI, A., et al (1994) Reliability and validity of the Personality Functioning Scale (PFS). *Journal of Personality Disorders,* 8, pp 111-120

MARLOWE, M., O'NEILL-BYRNE, K., LOWE-PONSFORD, F., et al (1996) The borderline syndrome index: a validation study using the personality assessment schedule. *British Journal of Psychiatry,* 168, pp 72-75

NORRIS, M. (1983) Changes in patients during treatment at Henderson Hospital therapeutic community during 1977-1981. *British Journal of Medical Psychology*, 56, pp 135-143

NORTON, K (1992) Personality disordered individuals: the Henderson Hospital model of treatment. *Criminal Behavior and Mental Health*, 2, pp 180-191

NORTON, K. & DOLAN, B (1995) Assessing change in personality disorder. *Current Opinion in Psychiatry*, 8, pp 371-375

RAPOPORT, R. (1960) *Community as Doctor*. London: Tavistock

REED, J. (1994) *Report of the Working Group on Psychopathic Disorder*. London: Department of Health/Home Office

REMINGTON, G. J & BOOK, H (1993) Discriminative validity of the Borderline Syndrome Index. *Journal of Personality Disorders*, 7, pp 312-319

# Cost-offset following specialist treatment of severe personality disorders

B. M. Dolan, F. M. Warren, D. Menzies and K. Norton

*Psychiatric Bulletin*
*(1996) 20, pp 413-417*

Service usage of 24 patients with a personality disorder was establish for one year pre-treatment and one year post-treatment via a prospective survey of the patients, their original referrer and their general practitioner. The average annual cost of psychiatric and prison services (calculated from extra-contractual referrals (ECR) tariffs and Home Office data) was £13,966 pre-treatment compared to £1,308 post-treatment, representing a cost-offset of £12,658 per patient per year. The average cost of the specialist admission was £25,641. Thus the cost to the Nation for treating these personality disordered patients in a tertiary treatment resource would be recouped within two years and represent a saving thereafter.

## INTRODUCTION

In some areas of psychotherapy there remains a paucity of adequate research into treatment outcome (Holmes, 1994; Marks, 1994). However, research evidence demonstrates good outcome of therapeutic community treatment for personality disordered patients in terms of psychiatric, psychological and behavioural changes (Dolan & Coid, 1993). Indeed, the recent joint Department of Health/Home Office committee on Services for Mentally Disordered Offenders (Reed, 1994) acknowledged that studies of therapeutic communities showed the most promising results of any form of treatment for psychopathic disorder (p.16) and recommended that more such units be provided (p. 43).

In light of this it is surprising that the scepticism regarding the treatability of personality disordered patients remains and that specialist psychotherapeutic treatments are often regarded as an expensive luxury

(Marks, 1994). In the climate of cost-awareness which now dominates the National Health Service (NHS), the onus is clearly on those services which can effect lasting improvement in their patients' psychological condition (i.e. beyond the period of actual treatment), to demonstrate the fact and to evaluate such treatment in financial terms.

Patients suffering with personality disorder place a high demand on health, as well as social and criminal justice, services which tend to be 'sucked in' in a reactive and unproductive way (Perry et al, 1987). One reason is that such patients typically fail to engage in or derive benefit from therapy and the severity of the behavioural (often antisocial) component of their disorder means they may not be adequately and safely treated in out-patient settings, or even day-hospital facilities which do not provide continuous support and/or supervision. Many have long histories of repeated contracts with psychiatric, social, forensic, penal and probation services which, because they represent incomplete or inadequate treatments do not confer lasting benefit; indeed many patients with personality disorders learn new aberrant coping strategies in such settings, including inappropriate dependence on professional carers.

Their antisocial and destructive behaviour often leads them to be seen as less deserving of health care service provision. This view may be especially prevalent when budgets are limited and the use of resources has to be closely monitored and rationalised. But refusing to fund treatment for such patients is a false economy, even if viewed solely in financial terms, since spontaneous remission of severe personality disorders is uncommon and untreated a patient will continue to remain a burden to professionals. In spite of this some purchasing Health Authorities, in apparent ignorance of the existing high costs of treating this group of patients, do not believe that additional financial outlay (in the form of expert, tertiary level, in-patient resources) is cost beneficial. This may be because the actual financial costs of the service usage of personality disordered people have rarely been quantified. However, in an earlier study (Menzies *et al*, 1993) we showed that a single cohort of 29 personality disordered patients admitted to Henderson Hospital service used a total of £423,115 worth of psychiatric and prison services in the one year prior to their admission. We extrapolated from earlier descriptive research data which showed a 40% reduction in service usage post-treatment and suggested that the initial cost of specialist treatment would be outweighed by the projected cost offset from this reduction over the ensuing four years.

Subsequently, we have had the opportunity to follow that same cohort of patients for one year following their discharge from treatment and have been able to calculate the actual service costs.

## THE STUDY

The sample in the initial study was 29 consecutive admissions to Henderson Hospital (which has 29 beds) in May 1992. Data on mental health and forensic service usage in the one year prior to their admission to Henderson Hospital were collected retrospectively from case notes and survey questionnaires (Menzies *et al,* 1993).

One year after discharge from treatment a brief questionnaire was sent to 29 patients their original referrers and their current general practitioners (GPs), asking for details of service usage since leaving Henderson Hospital. Information was returned from at least one professional source for 24 patients (73%) who formed the follow-up sample. Data came from the referrer only in ten cases (42%), the GP only in seven cases (29%) and from both professionals in seven cases (29%). In seven cases (29%) service usage data were also supplied by the patient. There was no difference in the figures for service usage when the source of information was the referrer, the GP or both, however, two patients gave information about receiving private counselling which was not recorded by their referrer or GP.

Twenty-three of the 24 subjects had completed the personality diagnostic questionnaire (PDQ-R; Hyler & Reider, 1987) on referral to Henderson Hospital. This is a self-report assessment of DSM-III-R personality disorder and thus susceptible to over-diagnosis. However, subjects showed multiple morbidity and met a mean of 6.04 (s.d=2.25) PDQ-R personality disorder criteria each. The most prevalent PDQ-R diagnosis was borderline personality disorder in 74% of subjects.

Costs of psychiatric in-patient, out-patient and day-patient services were calculated from extra-contractual referrals (ECR) tariffs provided by the four Thames Regional Health Authorities. Initial costs were calculated using 1992/3 tariffs and follow-up costs using 1993/4 tariffs.

*In-patient general psychiatry tariffs*
The average daily tariff for a general acute psychiatric in-patient bed across the Thames Regions was £153.20 for 1992/3 and £179 in 1993/4. (The daily bed tariff for Henderson Hospital was reduced from £111 to £110 in

the same period). The average daily bed cost of the Close Supervision Units in 1992/3 was £173.

*Out-patient general psychiatry tariffs*
Two calculations of out-patient costs were made. If a patient reported only 'having seen a psychiatrist' we judged this, conservatively, to mean having been assessed and offered one appointment. The average cost of such treatment was £179 in 1992/3 and £244 in 1973/4. If a patient reported having had 'individual therapy' of any type, but did not specify for how many sessions, we costed this using the figures for an assessment plus eight appointments. The average figure for a treatment package calculated in this way was £586 in 1992/3 and £790 in 1993/4. Day hospital costs were £71 and £70 per day respectively.

*Prison costs*
Prison costs were taken from the Home Office figures for 1991 (HMSO, 1991). The average cost of a week in a British adult prison was £386 (range £238-744).

**FINDINGS**

Table 1 presents a summary of mean psychiatric and prison service costs incurred by the 24 patients in the year prior to their admission. Costs in the year after admission are shown in Table 2.

*In-patient costs*
In the year prior to treatment 17 subjects (81%) had been in-patients (for a total of 1568 days) compared with three (1.25%) in the year following treatment (for a total of 73 days). One of these patients was readmitted to Henderson Hospital. Two patients (8%) had also been in Close Supervision Units for a total of 140 days before admission; however, none of the 24 subjects had been held in a secure unit in the year following treatment. Thus, the cumulative annual in-patient costs pre-treatment were £264,438 compared with £19,462 post-treatment.

**Table 1.  Service usage in the year before admission to Henderson 24 patients at 1992/3 tariffs**

| SERVICE | UNITS | N patients | N units | Unit mean | TOTAL COST |
|---|---|---|---|---|---|
| In-patient beds | day | 17 | 1568 | £ 153.2 | £ 240, 218 |
| Secure psychiatric beds | day | 2 | 140 | £ 173 | £ 24, 220 |
| Out-patient assessments | each | 6 | 6 | £ 179 | £ 1, 074 |
| Out-patient therapy | episode | 12 | 12 | £ 586 | £ 7, 032 |
| Day hospital | day | 3 | 404 | £ 71 | £ 28, 684 |
| Prison | week | 4 | 88 | £ 386 | £ 33, 968 |
| TOTAL COSTS | | | | | £ 335, 196 |
| COST PER PATIENT | | | | | £ 13, 966 |

**Table 2.  Service usage in the one year following admission 24 patients at 1993/4 tariffs**

| SERVICE | UNITS | N patients | N units | Unit mean | TOTAL COST |
|---|---|---|---|---|---|
| In-patient beds | day | 3 | 73 | £ 179 | £ 13,962 |
| Henderson Hospital | day | 1 | 50 | £ 110 | £ 5,500 |
| Out-patient assessments | each | 2 | 2 | £ 166 | £ 322 |
| Out-patient therapy | episode | 12 | 12 | £ 790 | £ 9,480 |
| Day hospital | day | 1 | 28 | £ 70 | £ 1,960 |
| TOTAL COSTS | | | | | £ 31,390 |
| COST PER PATIENT | | | | | £ 1,308 |

Six (25%) patients were reported as having had an out-patient assessment in the year before admission and two afterwards (8%). Twelve (50%) patients had out-patient treatment in the year before admission and the same number had out-patient treatment afterwards. Three residents (12.5%) had attended a day hospital for a total of 404 days before treatment and one (4.1%) had attended for 28 days at follow-up. The cumulative annual out-patient costs pre-treatment were £36,790 compared with £11,928 post-treatment.

### Prison costs
Four (17%) residents had been in custody in the previous year for a total of 88 weeks at a cost of £33,968. None of the 24 patients were reported as being in custody in the year following treatment.

### Total cost offset
Overall the total annual costs of prison and psychiatric service usage by these 24 patients was reduced from £335,196 (£13,966 per person) in the year before treatment to £31,390 (£1,308 per person) in the year following treatment. This represented a total cost-offset of £303,806 which is an average cost-offset of £12,658 per patient.

### Length of stay and cost of Henderson Hospital treatment
The 24 residents were in treatment at Henderson Hospital for an average of 231 days (range=1-365). The Henderson Hospital bed tariff at that time was £111 per day, thus the average treatment episode of Henderson Hospital for this cohort cost £25,641.

## COMMENT

In accord with research on personality disordered patients in the USA (Perry *et al* 1987), the 24 patients in this study had used a considerable amount of health and prison services in the year before admission at Henderson Hospital, at an estimated mean cost per patient of £13,966 (a total annual health care cost pre-treatment of £335,196). Overall there was a major reduction in service usage for the 24 patients following specialist in-patient treatment, to £1,308 per patient, which represented an average cost-offset of £12,658. If this reduction in service usage is maintained than the initial cost of the admission to Henderson Hospital (£25,641) would be recouped within just over two years and could be construed as a financial saving (to the

Nation) thereafter. However, this saving may be no consolation to the individual purchasers given the current funding system. Any purchaser financially supporting a referral to Henderson Hospital (or another similarly funded tertiary service) will not 'save' money from their own budget, even when treatment is successful, since the cost of the existing local purchaser-provider contract will not be diminished because of what amounts to an additional extra-contractual specialist referral.

However, appropriate and successful tertiary treatment may at least obviate the need for a further call on the ECR budget in the following year. Supra-regional funding of tertiary level treatment centres, such as Henderson Hospital, would save those 'unfortunate' purchasers, who have patients with such special needs from the 'penalty' of supporting their tertiary referral or ECR. Such a funding mechanism might remove disincentives to refer, since it seems all too common that financial considerations trump clinical need (Dolan *et al*, 1994).

This study assesses costs using average figures derived from data supplied by the four Thames Regional Health Authorities which provide only a rough guide to national charges, although 75% of Henderson Hospital patients come from those four regions. The use of retrospective case note information together with patients' and referrers' self-reports (for the first stage) and survey data from patient, referrer and GP (for the second stage) may have led to inaccuracies. In only 29% of cases was follow-up information verified by two professionals. However, the absence of any national (or even regional) system to identify hospital admissions of individuals makes cross checking for missing data impossible. The health care costs presented will be an underestimate of true costs since treatment via a GP or casualty department was not included. However, the under-representation of service use may equally influence the pre-treatment and follow-up figures, hence both will be underestimates of total costs involved that year. It is also possible that the year prior to admission to any tertiary treatment centre is not typical, the decision to refer a patient may reflect a worsening of their condition or a perception of an inappropriately high demand on local (secondary) services. As it cannot be simply assumed that each year will see the same level of demand on such services, further long-term research is required. This study measured only the health and penal service cost offset and did not attempt to measure cost-benefit which would have required a much fuller and more detailed financial profile, including past and future employment and tax payment status of patients.

We were unable to trace five (17%) of our original sample of 29 patients. It is possible that those five patients had a worse outcome in terms of service usage than those we were able to follow up. If the patient returned to the original referring catchment area, it would be likely that a referrer or GP would be interested in communicating a poor outcome of tertiary service input when requested to do so! However, some patients move on to new territory after treatment for a variety of reasons, including the maintenance of a peripatetic lifestyle. In such instances referrers and GPs may have replied because they had lost contact and possibly felt relief that their patient was no longer in touch. Other 'poor outcomes' which may not have prevented contact with the original referrer could have been re-hospitalisation elsewhere, imprisonment or death (a recent audit study showed that three of a cohort of 128 untreated referrals had committed suicide and one was a victim of homicide within a year of unsuccessful referral to Henderson Hospital.

Despite these caveats the study demonstrates a significant reduction in overall service usage which is financially quantifiable. If the benefit also includes entry or re-entry into paid employment then there are additional financial implications and cost-benefits. However, in presenting this outcome data based on sterling, the psychological and social benefits to the patient and his or her family and friends should not be forgotten or minimsed. There is additional research from Henderson Hospital which demonstrates the behavioural and psychological benefits of treatment (Copas *et al,* 1984; Dolan *el al,* 1992), many of which will not be readily or meaningfully translated in financial terms.

## REFERENCES

DOLAN, B. & COID, J. (1993) *Psychopathic and Anti-social Personality Disorders: Treatment and Research Issues.* London: Gaskell.

DOLAN, B., EVANS, C. & NORTON, K. (1994) Funding treatment for offender patients: do financial considerations trump clinical need? *Journal of Forensic Psychiatry,* 5, pp 263-272.

DOLAN, B.M., EVANS, C. & WILSON, J. (1992) Therapeutic community treatment for personality disordered adults: changes in neurotic symptomatology on follow-up. *International Journal of Social Psychiatry,* 38, pp 243-250.

HMSO (1991) *Report on the Work of the Prison Service: April 1990 – March 1991.* Cm 1724. London: HMSO.

HOLMES, J. (1994) Psychotherapy – A luxury the NHS can not afford? More expensive not to treat? *British Medical Journal,* 309, pp 1070-1071.

HYLER, S & REIDER, R. O. (1987*) Personality Diagnostic Questionnaire – Revisited.* New York: New York State Psychiatric Institute.

MARKS, I. (1994) Psychotherapy – A luxury the NHS can not afford? Unevaluated or inefficient approaches are hard to justify. *British Medical Journal,* 309, pp 1071-1072.

MENZIES, D., DOLAN, B & NORTON, K. (1993) Are short term savings worth long term costs? Funding treatment for personality disorders. *Psychiatric Bulletin,* 17, pp 517-519.

PERRY, J. C., LAVARI, P. W. & HOKE, L. (1987) A Markow model for predicting levels of psychiatric service use in borderline and anti-social personality disorders and bi-polar type II affective disorder. *Journal of Psychiatric Research,* 21, pp 213-232.

REED. J. (1994) *A Review of Services for Mentally Disordered Offenders and Others with Similar Needs: Report of the Sub-Committee on Psychopathic Disorder.* Department of Health/Home Office.

# An Innovative Outreach Service for People with Severe Personality Disorders:
## Patient Characteristics and Clinical Activities

Nicola Morant, Bridget Dolan, David Fainman
and Maggie Hilton

*The Journal of Forensic Psychiatry*
*(1999) Vol 10, No 1, pp 84-97*

This paper presents descriptive quantitative data on the first twelve months of operation of an innovative outreach service for people with severe personality disorders (SPD). Between November 1995 and November 1996 156 patients were referred to the service for out-patient treatment, in-patient preparatory work, post in-patient follow up and advice on management. The psychological and psychiatric characteristics of these patients are described using a range of standardised self-report scales. Scores indicate high levels of personality disorders, especially borderline personality disorder and associated behavioural and social problems. The various clinical activities of the service are described. These include the provision of individual and group psychotherapies, referrals for specialist in-patient admission and the provision of specialist advice on management to local referrers. Evidence suggests that the service is successfully achieving its aims in providing a specialist community service for people with SPD, but that current resourcing levels limit its ability to fully respond to service demands.

## INTRODUCTION

People with personality disorders (PD) typically manifest a range of emotional, interpersonal and behavioural problems. They may find the maintenance of long-term relationships difficult and lead chaotic lives punctuated by episodes of self harm, drug and alcohol abuse, and suicide attempts. Casey (1998) estimates that approximately 4% of the adult population suffer from SPD. However, the definition and assessment of the severity of personality disorders is contentious (Norton & Dolan, 1995; Tyrer & Johnson, 1996). It is widely recognised that multiple co-morbid PD diagnoses are common and that, despite its imprecision, severe personality disorder (SPD) is a useful term in the assessment of psychopathology, choice of treatment and evaluation of treatment outcome (Kernberg, 1984; Norton & Hinshelwood, 1996). Several authors have produced findings which suggests that 'breadth' of personality disorders (as measured by the number of PD diagnoses) can be equated with severity (Dolan & Coid, 1993; Dolan et al, 1995; Tyrer & Johnson, 1996). For example, the number of PD diagnoses increases with the level of security of the settings from which samples are drawn (Dolan et al, 1995), and there is a strong correlation between the number of PD diagnoses and levels of social, psychological and occupational disturbance (Dolan & Coid, 1993). People with SPD are not only over-represented in the criminal justice system, but are also intensive users of health and mental health services (Tyrer, 1988). They often require services in response to crises, but may be difficult to engage in long-term management strategies. Treatment is frequently complicated by sporadic attendance, over dependence and 'acting out' (Norton & McGauley, 1998). As a result, the treatability of personality disorders is frequently doubted by clinicians, and following a survey which detected pejorative attitudes amongst clinicians, Lewis and Appleby (1988) described SPD clients as 'the patients psychiatrists dislike'.

Against this context of therapeutic pessimism and lack of appropriate resources, Henderson Hospital therapeutic community provides specialist treatment for personality disordered clients using a combination of group psychotherapy and sociotherapeutic strategies. This residential treatment has been shown to be clinically effective (Copas et al, 1984; Dolan et al, 1997; Norris, 1995), cost efficient (Dolan et al, 1996) and to reduce service usage (Whiteley, 1970). Based on this demonstrable success and its long history of treating personality disordered clients, Henderson Hospital established a specialist out-patient service for people with SPD in 1995. This was in response to concerns about the national paucity of services for this difficult patient group, as recognised in a government commissioned review of services for psychopathic disorders (Reed, 1994). This report highlighted a need for the development of a more comprehensive network of out-patients services for SPD patients, and recommended that future service should employ minimal levels of security and treat patients as close to their place of residence as possible. The establishment of HOST was also motivated by a multi-disciplinary audit study conducted at Henderson Hospital which identified a perceived need for aftercare following in-patient admission amongst current and ex-patients and referring clinicians (Dolan & Murch, 1993 unpublished).

Henderson Outreach Service Team (HOST) was set up to provide a multi-disciplinary peripatetic assessment and treatment service for SPD patients resident in five health authorities in the South Thames Region, an area of population approximately 2,711,000 (Institute of Health Services Management, 1996). As a tertiary level service HOST accepts referrals from members of Community Mental Health Teams within the catchment area. The service does not normally accept referrals of patients who are subject to legal restrictions under the Mental Health Act or who have moderate to severe learning disabilities.

The stated aims of HOST are to provide specialist treatment for people with SPD and to translate the successful in-patient 'therapeutic community' strategies of psychotherapy and sociotherapy, (and related principles of democracy, reality confrontation, permissiveness) into treatment in out-patient settings. Group treatment and a limited amount of individual treatment is provided, both as a 'before and aftercare' service for the 'parent' specialist in-patient unit (Henderson Hospital), and as an alternative to in-patient care. In addition, the service aims to cascade expertise in the management of difficult clients to local teams. It provides a weekly supervision group for clinicians and joint working opportunities to support local Community Mental Health Teams (CMHTs) in managing personality disordered patients within their local facilities. The service currently employs 2.4 experienced clinical staff with trainings in clinical psychology, psychotherapy and psychiatry. The treatment philosophy which underpins HOST is unusual and innovative, and the service represents an exciting new development in specialist community-based services.

Building on an established tradition of research and internal audit at Henderson Hospital (Copas et al, 1984; Dolan & Murch, 1993 unpublished; Dolan et al, 1996; Dolan et al, 1997), on-going monitoring in the form of independently funded clinical audit has been built into the service from its inception. These investigations are part of the on-going audit and service development spiral in which a progression towards improved patient care is achieved through the monitoring and evaluation of clinical initiatives in response to recommendations and un-met need, and results are used to inform the evolution of future service developments (Gray et al, 1996). Given the innovative nature of the service, clinical audit during the early stages of service development is most useful if it takes a broader approach than that traditionally used in established services, where clinical procedures have been standardised and relevant service standards are already available. Thus, rather than relying on a single measure of 'quality', this audit evaluates the service from several different perspectives including treatment outcome, service usage, cost off-set, interface with primary and secondary level services, and evaluation of the service by local referrers and service users. These broader investigations have the scope for generalisation and the potential to inform national and international debate about service provision for this difficult client group.

This paper presents data on the clinical and demographic characteristics of patients referred to HOST in its first twelve months of operation, together with data on the clinical activities of the service during this period. The collation of this 'baseline' data provides the basis from which further service evaluations and developments can proceed.

## METHODOLOGY

A wide range of data was obtained from questionnaires, referral letters, case notes and a computerised clinical data base. All data were collected and analysed by the research psychologist responsible for conducting the clinical audit (NM). Questionnaires were sent to referrers and clients at the point of initial referral. Three separate questionnaires were used:-

*1.   A Psychological Self Report Questionnaire (completed by the patient).*
This includes several established rating scales which have been shown to be useful indicators of current problems and treatment outcomes with personality disordered patients in previous research at Henderson Hospital and elsewhere (Dolan et al, 1997; Edell, 1984; Hurt et al, 1984; Norris, 1985; Norton & Dolan, 1995). The following scales were included:

*The Personality Diagnostic Questionnaire, Version 4 (PDQ-4) (Hyler et al, 1988; Hyler, 1994 unpublished).*
This instrument assesses the presence of criteria for the 10 sub-types of personality disorder described in DSM-4. A cut-off score of 30 or more is suggested by the author as indicating a substantial likelihood of significant personality disorder (Hyler, personal communication). A more useful indicator of the severity of disorder may be the number of PD diagnoses generated by this instrument (Dolan & Coid, 1993; Dolan et al, 1995).

*Borderline Syndrome Index (BSI) (Conte et al, 1980).*
This is a 52 item forced choice scale designed to assess borderline psychopathology associated with both borderline personality disorder and borderline personality organisation (Kernberg, 1967). Dolan et al (1997) have found that the point of clinical significance on this scale (which differentiates between non-clinical and clinical samples) is 20.

*Multi-Impulsivity Scale (MIS) (Searle, Evans & Dolan, 1998).*
This scale scores the frequency of impulsively doing or wanting to do eleven actions typically seen in people with a diagnosis of personality disorder. Frequencies are recording using six point Likert scales ranging from 'never' (1) to 'always' (6). Actions include self harm (overdosing, binge eating, cutting or burning); drug and alcohol misuse; and various forms of violent

and anti-social behaviour (fire setting, sexual behaviour, violence to others or to property, shoplifting and gambling).

*Irritability, Depression and Anxiety Scale (IDA) (Snaith et al, 1978).*
This instrument produces scores on four sub-scales: Depression, Anxiety, Inward irritability and Outward irritability.
Rosenberg Self Esteem Inventory (Rosenberg, 1965).
Possible scores on this commonly used scale of self worth range from 0 to 6, with a high score indicating low self worth.

2. *A 'Social History' form (completed by the patient).*
This three page questionnaire asks about patients' domestic circumstances, employment, contact with psychiatric and social services, forensic histories, alcohol and drug use, and incidents of self harm.

3. *'Referral Information' Form (completed by the referrer).*
This asks referrers to report on the demographic details of their clients, their present psychological state, and their previous psychiatric and forensic histories. Overlap with some of the information obtained on the social history form enhances the completeness of the data set. Where there are discrepancies between data provided by patients and referrers, it was decided to use patient data as the more accurate measure of current social and behavioural characteristics.

## RESULTS

In its first twelve months of operation (November 1995 to November 1996), 156 patients were referred to the service. These people had a mean age of 31.5 years (minimum 18, maximum 55) and were equally split in terms of sex (47% female, 53% male). Response rates for the scales included in the self report questionnaires completed by patients at the point of referral ranged from 65% to 70%. Referral Information Forms completed by referrers were returned for 93% of patients.

## 1. *Description of the Patient Group*

Data collated from self reports 'social history' forms and 'referral information' indicate high levels of behavioural and social problems amongst the patient group. Table 1 shows levels of various behavioural indicators of disturbance and characteristics associated with social deprivation and isolation in the twelve months prior to referral for the 148 patients for whom data is available. These characteristics are similar to those reported in patients admitted to the parent in-patient unit (Henderson Hospital), although slightly lower levels of previous in-patient admissions and suicide attempts are found (Norton, 1992). Self mutilation (66%) usually takes the form of cutting (most commonly of the arms or wrists), but burning and hitting are also reported. Non-prescribed drug use (46%) involves most frequently cannabis, followed by amphetamines, 'ecstasy' and cocaine. In an open question about the nature of their current problems, patients typically report depression, self-esteem problems, strained relationships with family members, anger management problems, feelings of loss of control, eating, drug and alcohol problems and financial problems. Two people had been in prison in the year prior to referral, and ten were on probation at the time of referral. In addition to 55% of patients who live on their own, 17% report transient living arrangements at the point of referral, in the form of hostel, bed and breakfast or hospital accommodation.

**Table 1: Behavioural and Social Characteristics of HOST Referrals in 12 Months**

Prior to Referral (N=148)

| Characteristics | Number of Referrals (%) |
|---|---|
| Living Alone | 82 (55%) |
| Not Employed | 132 (89%) |
| Psychiatric In-patient Treatment | 89 (60%) |
| Drug Abuse | 68 (46%) |
| Self Mutilation | 98 (66%) |
| Taken Overdose | 84 (57% |
| Alcohol Misuse | 67 (45%) |
| Attempted Suicide | 58 (39%) |

**Table 2: PDQ-4 Diagnoses of Personality Disorder:**

Percentages of the sample scoring within the clinical range (N=102)

| Personality Disorder Category | % of sample scoring within the clinical range |
|---|---|
| Antisocial | 44% |
| Avoidant | 79% |
| Borderline | 86% |
| Dependent | 42% |
| Histrionic | 18% |
| Narcissistic | 19% |
| Obsessive-Compulsive | 50% |
| Paranoid | 70% |
| Schizoid | 33% |
| Schizotypal | 47% |
| Total PD Score | 89% |

**Table 3: Mean scores on self report measures at the point of initial referral (N=106)**

| Scale | Mean (sd) | % of sample scoring within the clinical range |
|---|---|---|
| Borderline Syndrome Index (BSI) | 30.8 (10.43) | 83% |
| Rosenberg Self-esteem Inventory | 4.89 (1.56) | - |
| Irritability, Depression and Anxiety Scale (IDA): | | |
| Depression | 8.5 (2.87) | 80% |
| Anxiety | 8.1 (2.49) | 49% |
| Inward Irritability | 6.4 (2.48) | 58% |
| Outward Irritability | 6.8 (2.26) | 39% |

Results of the self-report instruments used to measure psychological and psychiatric characteristics of the patient group are shown in Tables 2 and 3. Table 2 shows scores on the PDQ-4 which indicate that 89% of the sample score above the clinical cut-off point of 30 for some form of personality disorder, with an average total score of 38.9. High levels of co-morbidity of PD diagnoses are indicated with referrals scoring above the diagnostic cut-off point for an average of 4.9 personality disorders. The number of PD diagnoses is normally distributed and ranges from 0 to 9. Only 7% of the sample show either no PD or a single PD diagnosis. The most common specific personality disorders identified by the PDQ-4 are borderline, avoidant and paranoid personality disorders.

Mean scores on the Borderline Syndrome Index (BSI), Rosenberg Self-esteem Inventory, and Irritability, Depression and Anxiety Scale (IDA) are shown in Table 3. The mean score of 30.8 on the BSI compares to mean scores of 26.31 and 5.92 respectively for samples of psychiatric out-patients with a diagnosis of borderline personality disorder and normal controls reported by the authors of the scale (Conte et al, 1980). In comparison, a mean of 34.6 is reported in a sample of 70 personality disordered patients admitted to the parent in-patient unit at the point of referral (Dolan et al, 1997). On the Rosenberg Self-esteem inventory there is a mean score of 4.89, although the distribution of scores is skewed negatively, with 50% of cases scoring the maximum of 6. This is indicative of severe self esteem problems amongst this client group, especially when these findings are compared with mean scores for other groups. For example, Ingham et al (1986) report mean scores of 1.14 for non-clinical controls, 2.5 for patients with 'intermittent depression and other personality disorders', and 3.03 for patients with major depressive disorders. Mean scores on the IDA scale fall within the clinical ranges for all sub-scales except outwardly directed irritability, for which the mean score is within the 'borderline' range between clinical and non-clinical scores.

Scores on the Multi-Impulsivity Scale (MIS) indicating frequencies of wanting to do or doing various impulsive behaviours vary considerably both across the different actions and within the group of respondents. However, mis-using alcohol, binge eating and self harming were reported as the most commonly enacted impulses in the previous two months, with mean scores of 2.4, 2.2 and 2.2 respectively, corresponding to between 'occasionally' and 'sometimes' on the frequency scale. The most common actions which patients report having wanted to do were hitting someone or something, and self harming, with a mean frequency for each of these of between 'sometimes' and 'often' (3.14 for hitting and 3.2 for self harm).

2. Clinical activity in the first twelve months of operation

The reasons for which referrals to the service were made (as indicated in initial referral letters) are shown in Table 4.

**Table 4: Reasons for referral of 156 patients in the first year of the service**

| Reason for Referral | Number of Referrals (%) N=156 |
|---|---|
| Treatment:  With the outreach service | 86 (55%) |
| Either with the outreach service or at the  parent | 65 (42%) |
| specialist in-patient unit | 21 (13%) |
| Following failure to be selected for the in-patient unit | 10 (6%) |
| Following discharge from the in patient unit | 19 (12%) |
| Referral for advice on management | 13 (8%) |
| General referral (exact reason not specified) | 28 (18%) |

Nearly one fifth of referrals to the service (n=29, 18%) come via the parent specialist in-patient unit (following either discharge or selection failure). However, the majority of referrals (68%, n=106) are made without an explicit association with the in-patient unit, suggesting that the service also operates as an out-patient facility in its own right.  The vast majority of referrals are for some form of treatment, with explicit requests for management advice only constituting the smallest group of referrals.

Following referral, all 156 patients were offered a full assessment (including detailed clinical formulations and advice on future treatment strategies). Twenty-eight of these (18%) did not attend their initial appointments, and a further 16 (10%) did not complete the assessment.  The outcomes of the completed assessments conducted with the remaining 112 patients are shown in Table 5.

**Table 5: Outcome of assessments conducted with 112 patients**

| Outcome of Assessment | Number (%) N=112 |
|---|---|
| Treatment Provided: Individual treatment | 40 (36%) |
| Weekly psychotherapy group | 22 (20%) |
| Weekly art psychotherapy group | 14 (13%) |
| | 4 (3%) |
| Did not attend for treatment | 8 (7%) |
| Resources for treatment not available | 11 (10%) |
| Assessed as not suitable for treatment | 33 (29%) |
| Referred to parent specialist in-patient unit | 13 (11%) |
| Management advice provided to referrer | 7 (6%) |

In its first year of operation, the service provided some form of individual or group based treatment for one quarter of all its referrals, and over a third of those with whom a clinical assessment was completed (n=40). Of these forty people, eleven were referred following discharge from the parent specialist in-patient unit. For six of these patients, individual follow-up treatment was provided, using forms of psychodynamic psychotherapy, cognitive therapy and supportive working. The remaining five ex-inpatients entered weekly art or verbal psychotherapy groups. Thirteen of the people assessed by the service were referred to the parent specialist in-patient unit, and lack of resources precluded the provision of treatment for 11 patients. Of the 33 people assessed as not currently suitable for treatment with the service, analysis of case notes indicates that the most common reasons were the need for more containment, lack of commitment to engagement in therapy, and severe alcohol and drug problems which needed to be addressed prior to outreach treatment.

## DISCUSSION

The scores obtained on psychological self report scales for the first 156 referrals to this new service indicate a patient group manifesting high levels of personality disorder, specifically borderline personality disorder. High scores on the PDQ-4 and high co-morbidity of PD diagnoses suggest that

HOST patients fall towards the severe end of the spectrum of personality disorders. A range of clinically significant psychological problems including low self esteem, depression, anxiety, irritability and poor impulse control are also detected. These levels of psychopathology and behavioural disturbances mirror problems typically found in SPD patient groups and are problems associated with many of the Health of the Nation 'key areas'. They are also similar to, although slightly lower than, the levels of psychopathology detected in studies conducted at the parent in-patient unit (Dolan et al, 1994; Dolan et al; 1995, Dolan et al, 1997; Norton, 1992). HOST's patient group are also frequent users of other psychiatric services.

Data indicate that clinical activities in the first twelve months match the services' stated aims of providing a combination of preparatory and follow up treatment for a specialist in-patient unit, alternative out-patient group and individual treatment programmes, and management advice to local mental health teams working with people with SPD. The vast majority of referrals to HOST in the first year of the service were for some form of treatment. Although treatment was offered to nearly a third (n=48) of these referrals, with resource levels set at 2.4 whole time equivalent clinicians, the service was unable to provide treatment for 11 (10%) of the patients it assessed. This suggests, arguably, that even within twelve months of its establishment, demand for these forms of out-patient treatment for SPD patients outweighed HOST's ability to provide these services.

In its assessment and preparatory work for the parent in-patient unit (provided for 13 patients in the first 12 months), there are indications that HOST acts as a useful filter for a more expensive in-patient service. Although this is a small group from which few definitive conclusions can be drawn, nine of these thirteen people (69%) were successfully selected for admission to the in-patient unit. This compares to only one third of an equivalent group of patients who did not have any prior contact with the outreach service, and suggests that out-patient preparatory work may be beneficial in enhancing the likelihood of successful selection for the in-patient unit (a democratic therapeutic community environment). There are also some early indications that prior contact with HOST helps to prevent treatment drop-out from the in-patient unit. These 9 patients accepted for the in-patient unit stayed for 31 weeks on average. This compares to an average length of stay of 19 weeks for 31 patients from the same geographical area who were admitted to the in-patient unit without prior out-patient contact during the same time period. The fact that clinicians in the outreach service work sessionally at the in-patient unit may help in preparation for its intensive group-based culture by allowing potential patients to develop realistic expectations and encouraging the discussion of features or difficulties associated with this form of treatment.

However, these preliminary data also highlight some problematic areas in service provision which are the foci of current monitoring and service developments. Although the remit of HOST includes both treatment provision and advice / joint working with local CMHTs, the provision of treatment for only 40 of the 156 referrals merits some consideration. Partially, this is due to high levels of non-attendance. The largest group of non-attenders are patients who do not attend for the first appointment (18%). Ten percent of patients dropped out before the assessment period was completed and eight (17%) of the patients offered treatment with the service did not take this up. Comparisons of these patients with those who attended for treatment detect no demographic or psychiatric differences between the two groups. Relatively high rates of non attendance and difficulties of engagement are recognised problems amongst people with SPD and are therefore to be expected in this service (Norton & Hinshelwood, 1996; Vaglum et al, 1990). Whether these non-attendance rates are acceptable for a service such as this is a matter of debate for clinicians and service managers. However, the closer working relationships which HOST clinicians have developed with both the in-patient unit and local referring teams since this early data on the service was collected may help to generate referrals of clients who are well informed and motivated to engage with the treatment style of the service.

Another factor that has compromised treatment provision by HOST is the large proportion of referrals (29%) who are inappropriate for the service, usually due to a need for more containment or because of serious addiction problems. This issue is being addressed through the dissemination of clearer information for potential referrers about the remit and limitations of the service and the types of treatments it is able to offer. The success of this effort to generate more appropriate and specific referrals from local teams is being monitored as part of on-going clinical audit of the service, for which the data in this paper forms an initial baseline. A final factor compromising the amount of treatment HOST was able to provide in its first year is limited clinical resources. Although the use of group treatments has allowed the 2.4 whole time equivalent clinicians to treat many more people than on an individual basis, the service has struggled to respond adequately to the number of requests for treatment. In addition, the peripatetic nature of the service and time spent travelling between clinics across the catchment area has eroded the amount of time available for clinical work.

There is ample recognition of the paucity of appropriate networks of services for people with personality disorders both nationally (Reed, 1994), and within the South Thames (West) Region (Cohen et al, 1994 unpublished; Dolan & Murch, 1993 unpublished). Although treatment outcome data for the service is not yet available, the establishment of this service may constitute a timely and appropriate development, both locally and nationally. Data suggest that the service is meeting a need for out-patient treatments for SPD patients. In applying specialised clinical expertise in working with people with SPD to break cycles of dependency and crisis, it is to be hoped that the service provides treatment which is appropriate to the long-term needs of this patient group. Local CMHT services are often not geared to the specific needs of SPD patients and their clinicians may have little knowledge or experience of working successfully with this difficult client group. As an endorsement of the service's value in providing both treatment and advice to local teams, interviews with local referrers to the service conducted as part of this clinical audit suggest that local psychiatric teams value the specialised knowledge of its clinicians but would like the service to provide more direct on-going treatment for their clients.

Since the data for this paper was collected, a bid for 'top-sliced' funding to develop a national multi-centre service for the treatment of SPD based on the Henderson Hospital model has been successful. This will provide funding from 1998 for HOST to expand to a multi-disciplinary team of seven clinical staff who will provide services for SPD clients across the south east of England. With increased resources it will be possible to provide a more comprehensive out-patient treatment service for people with

SPD over a wider geographical area. Clinical audit data is currently being used to guide decisions about the future direction and remit of the service. This use of audit data in continued service development completes the audit loop, and constitutes an important first stage in developing an evidence-led service which is able to respond appropriately to clinical needs, and interface effectively within local mental health service networks.

## ACKNOWLEDGEMENTS
*This study is funded by a grant from South Thames Clinical Audits Programme.*

## REFERENCES

CASEY, P. (1988) The epidemiology of personality disorder. In Tyrer, P. (ed.) *Personality Disorder: Diagnosis, management and clinical care.* London: Wright.

CONTE, H. R., PLUNTCHIK, R., & JERRET, I. (1980) 'A self-report borderline scale: Discriminant validity and preliminary norms'. *Journal of Nervous and Mental Disease,* 168: pp 428-435.

COPAS, J., O'BRIAN, M., ROBERTS, J. & WHITELEY, S. (1984) 'Treatment outcome in personality disorder: the effect of social, psychological and behavioural variables'. *Personality and Individual Differences,* 5 (5): pp 565-573.

DOLAN, B. & COID, J (1993) *Psychopathic and Antisocial Personality Disorders: Treatment and research issues.* London: Gaskell.

DOLAN, B., EVANS, C. & NORTON, K. (1994) 'Funding treatment of offender patients with severe personality disorder: Do financial considerations trump clinical need?' *Journal of Forensic Psychiatry,* 5 (2) pp 263-274.

DOLAN, B., EVANS, C. & NORTON, K. (1995) 'Multiple axis-II diagnoses of personality disorder'. *British Journal of Psychiatry,* 166: pp 107-112.

DOLAN, B., WARREN, F. & NORTON, K. (1997) 'Change in borderline symptoms one year after therapeutic community treatment for severe personality disorder'. *British Journal of Psychiatry,* 171: pp 274-279.

DOLAN, B., WARREN, F., NORTON, K. & MENZIES, D. (1996) 'Cost off-set following therapeutic community treatment of personality disorder.' *Psychiatric Bulletin,* 20: pp 1-5.

EDELL, W. S. (1984) 'The Borderline Syndrome Index: Clinical validity and utility'. *Journal of Nervous and Mental Disease,* 172 (5): pp 254-63.

GRAY, M., KETTLES, A., SPENCE, A. & SMITH, G. (1996) 'Clinical audit in community mental health care'. *Mental Health Nursing,* 16 (5): pp 10-13.

HURT, S. W., HYLER, S. E., FRANCES, A., CLARKIN, J. F. & BRENT, R. (1984) 'Assessing borderline personality disorder with self-report, clinical interview or semi-structured interview'. *American Journal of Psychiatry,* 141: pp 1228-1231.

HYLER, S., REIDER, R. O., WILLIAMS, J. B., SPITZER, R. L.,

HENDLER, J. & LYONS, M. (1988) 'The Personality diagnostic Questionnaire: Development and preliminary results'. *Journal of Personality Disorders* 2: pp 229-237.

INSTITUTE OF HEALTH SERVICES MANAGEMENT (1996) *The IHSM Health and Social Services Year Book 1996/97.* London: IHSM.

INGHAM, J., KREITMAN, N., MCMILLER, P., SASHIDHARAN, S. & SURTEES, P. (1986) 'Self-esteem, vulnerability and psychiatric disorder in the community'. *British Journal of Psychiatry* 148: pp 375-385.

KERNBERG, O. (1967) 'Borderline personality organisation'. *Journal of the American Psychoanalytic Association* 15: pp 641-685.

KERNBERG, O. (1984) *Severe Personality Disorders: Psychotherapeutic strategies.* London: Yale University Press.

LEWIS, G. & APPLEBY, L. (1988) 'Personality disorders: the patients psychiatrists dislike'. *British Journal of Psychiatry* 153: pp 44-49.

NORRIS, M. (1985) 'Changes in patients during treatment at Henderson Hospital therapeutic community during 1977-1981'. *British Journal of Medical Psychology* 56: pp 135-43.

NORTON, K. (1992) 'Personality disordered individuals: The Henderson Hospital model of treatment'. *Criminal Behaviour and Mental Health* 2 (2): pp 80-191.

NORTON, K. & DOLAN, B. (1995) 'Assessing change in personality disorder'. *Current Opinion in Psychiatry* 8: pp 371-375.

NORTON, K. & HINSHELWOOD, R. D. (1996) 'Severe personality disorder: treatment issues and selection for in-patient psychotherapy'. *British Journal of Psychiatry* 168: pp 723-731.

NORTON, K. & MCGAULEY, G. (1998) *Counselling Difficult Clients.* London: Sage.

REED, J. (1994) *Report of the Department of Health and Home Office Working Group on Psychopathic Disorder.* London: HMSO.

ROSENBERG, M. (1965) *Society and the Adolescent Self Image.* New York: Princeton University Press.

SEARLE, Y., EVANS, C. & DOLAN, B. (1998, in press) 'Two new tools for the assessment of multi-impulsivity: The 'MIS' and the 'CAM''. *European Review of Eating Disorders.*

SNAITH, R. P., CONSTANTOPOULOS, A., JARDINE, M. & MCGUFFIN, P. (1978) 'A clinical scale for the self assessment of irritability'. *British Journal of Psychiatry* 132: pp 164-71.

TYRER, P. (1988) *Personality Disorder: Diagnosis, Management and Care.* London: Wright.

TYRER, P. & JOHNSON, T. (1996) Establishing the severity of personality disorder. *American Journal of Psychiatry,* 153 (12): pp 1593-97.

VAGLUM, P., FRIIS, S., IRION, T., JOHNS, S., KARTERUD, S., LARSEN, F. & VAGLUM, S. (1990) 'Treatment response of severe and non-severe personality disorders in a therapeutic community day unit.' *Journal of Personality Disorders* 2: pp 161-172.

WHITELEY, J. S. (1970) The response of psychopaths to a therapeutic community. *British Journal of Psychiatry* 116: pp 517-29.

# ANNOTATED BIBLIOGRAPHY

## 1980-2000

# Bibliography of Writings on Henderson Hospital

## 1980-2000

### THE CLINICAL PROGRAMME

◆ Kerr, I. (2000) **Vygotsky, activity theory and the therapeutic community: a further paradigm?** *Therapeutic Communities: International Journal for Therapeutic and Supportive Organisations* Vol. 21 (1)

◆ Norton, K. (1997) **Inpatient Psychotherapy: integrating the other 23 hours.** *(Comment) Current Medical Literature,* May, Vol. 8: No.2: pp 31-37
*An emphasis of the advantage that residential therapeutic communities have of being able to observe and use therapeutically, the time other than the formal psychotherapy time offered to an individual patient.*

◆ Dolan, B. (1997) **A Community based TC: The Henderson Hospital.** In *Therapeutic Communities for Offenders* Edited by Cullen E, Jones L, Woodward R. pp 47-74. John Wiley & Sons Ltd.
*The history of Henderson Hospital and review of the treatment programme, resident characteristics and research evidence including psychological, behavioural and cost-offset approaches to evaluation.*

◆ Warren, F. & Dunstan, F. (1997) **Thinkers and feelers.** *Counselling News,* March 1997, pp 32-33
*A short descriptive piece about the clinical model, history and outcomes of Henderson Hospital for its 50th anniversary year.*

◆ Warren, F. & Dolan, B. (1996) **Research Update. Therapeutic communities and personality disorder.** Forensic Update 46: 26-35
*Reviews the outcome research into therapeutic community treatment for personality disorders.*

♦ Norton, K. & Dolan, B. (1995) **Acting out and the institutional response.** *Journal of Forensic Psychiatry* Vol.6 (2): pp 317-332
*The response of institutions to self-damaging, impulsive and violent behaviours often serves to perpetuate the behaviour and inadvertently remove the potential for behavioural and psychological change. The paper examines how the interactions between individuals and 'institutions' may be understood and re-organised so that individuals may psychologically mature and learn from the experience rather than have maladaptive behaviours ignored or reinforced.*

♦ Norton, K. (1992) **Personality disordered individuals: the Henderson Hospital model of treatment.** *Criminal Behaviour and Mental Health,* Vol.2: pp 180-191
*A description of the structural and therapeutic ingredients of Henderson's Therapeutic Community model and its degree of applicability to other settings, especially for those patients requiring higher levels of security.*

♦ Norton, K. (1992) **A culture of enquiry its preservation or loss.** *Therapeutic Communities* Vol.1(1): pp 3-26
*Examines Tom Main's contribution to therapeutic community theory and practice. Main's concept a 'culture of enquiry' is described in the context of Henderson Hospital and the importance of staff in maintaining the culture and structure of the community is discussed.*

♦ Norton, K. (1990) **The significance and importance of the Therapeutic Community working practice.** *International Journal of Therapeutic Communities.* Vol.11 (2): pp 67-76
*Describes the Therapeutic Community's emphasis on process rather than outcome ('means' more than 'ends') in the light of other non-therapeutic community theoretical perspectives including that of James Hillman on the nature of 'working' itself.*

♦ Dolan, B.M., Polley, K., Allen, R., Norton K. (1991) **Addressing racism in psychiatry: Is the Therapeutic Community approach applicable?** *International. Journal of Social Psychiatry.* Vol.37: pp 71-79
*Possible reasons for the under-representation of black clients in psychotherapy are discussed and it is argued that the Therapeutic Community model of treatment (or aspects of it) provides a potential for a less racist service approach. However, despite the ideological suitability of the therapeutic community model, practical changes are*

*still necessary, before Henderson Hospital can adequately meet the needs of clients in a multi-cultural Britain.*

♦   Whiteley, J.S. (1980) **The Henderson Hospital: A community study**
*International Journal of Therapeutic Communities* Vol. 1(1): pp 38-57
*An essential guide to the history and development of Henderson Hospital from 1947 to 1980.*

## See also these earlier key papers

♦   Mahoney, N. (1979)   **My Stay and Change at the Henderson Therapeutic Community.** Chapter in: Hinshelwood, R. and Manning, N. (eds.) *Therapeutic Communities: Reflections and Progress:* pp76-87, Routledge, London
*A moving account of one resident's 10   month stay at Henderson with personal reflections from his selection interview, through his treatment and after discharge.*

♦   Azu-Okeke, O. (1972)   **An appraisal of the dynamics of a Therapeutic Community - The Henderson.***British Journal of Social Psychiatry* Vol.6 (1): pp 26-37
*Focuses upon the sociological aspects of TC treatment and discusses how, to sustain the community,   interdependent functioning is required which can be threatened by functional autonomy of community members.*

♦   Jones, M. (1956) **Industrial Rehabilitation of mental patients still in hospital.** *The Lancet* Nov. Vol.10: pp 985-986
*A description of the original industrial rehabilitation programme and its outcome for 100 patients at six month follow-up.*

♦   Jones, M. (1956)   **The concept of a Therapeutic Community.** *American Journal of Psychiatry*, Vol.112: pp 647-650
*Discussion of the importance of staff-patient relationships and roles in the TC concept, the centrality of the community meeting and the application of some general TC principles to other settings.*

♦   Jones, M. (1946) **Rehabilitation of forces neurosis patients to civilian life.** *British Medical Journal* April Vol. 6: pp 533-535

*Details the staffing and activities of the P.O.W. neurosis unit established by Jones at Dartford in May 1945.*

♦ Jones, M. (1942) **Group Psychotherapy.** *British Medical Journal* Vol. 2: pp 276-278
*A fascinating early account of the development and efficacy of group treatment methods with soldiers suffering form 'effort-syndrome' and the role of nurses within the treatment unit.*

# SPECIFIC ASPECTS OF
# THE TREATMENT PROGRAMME

♦ Birch, S.L., Dunstan, F. & Warren, F. (1999) **Democratisation, reality confrontation, permissiveness, and communalism. Themes or anachronisms? An Examination of Therapeutic Agents Using Factor Analysis. Journal of Therapeutic Communities.** *Therapeutic Communities*, Vol.20: No.1: pp 43-59
*This paper attempts to explore the four tenets of therapeutic community working proposed by Rapoport by subjecting his original questionnaire and a new questionnaire derived by clinicians at Henderson Hospital to factor analysis. The results did not support either questionnaire measuring the four principles.*

♦ Norton, K., Bulmer, R. & Suddards, L. (1999) **Managing change in a therapeutic community: every silver lining has a cloud.** *Therapeutic Communities: International Journal for Therapeutic and Supportive Organisations.* Vol. 20(1): 3-10

♦ Gordon, D. Giles, S. (1999) **From May to November: A six month group for women survivors of childhood abuse.** *Group Analysis* Vol. 32 (4): pp 496-505
*A discussion of a specialist group run in the early activities of Henderson Outreach Service Team (HOST).*

♦ Morant, N., Dolan, B., Fainman, D, & Hilton, M. (1999) **An Innovative Outreach Service for People With Severe Personality Disorders: Patient Characteristics and Clinical Activities.**
*Journal of Forensic Psychiatry*: Vol. 10: No 1: pp 84-97
*A descriptive report on the first twelve months activity of the Henderson Outreach Service Team (HOST) including the psychological and demographic characteristics of patients referred to the service in this time. The paper highlights the demand for services of this kind.*


♦ Norton, K.R.W. (1998) **Joining and Leaving: Processing Separation, Loss and Re-Attachment.** In *Therapeutic communities: past, present and future:* Eds. Haigh, R and Campling, P. London: Jessica Kingsley Publishers.
*Addresses the issues of clients engaging and disengaging from treatment in the therapeutic community and discusses the attempts made by Henderson Hospital to facilitate these processes.*


♦ Esterhuyzen, A. & Winterbotham, M. (1998) **Surfing the interface: How to make a welfare group a microcosm of therapeutic community functioning.** *Therapeutic Communities*: Vol.19: No.4: pp 295-305
*Access to housing, financial support and other social necessities is particularly difficult for those labelled with mental health problems. At Henderson Hospital residents are supported to make these arrangements for themselves throughout their stay and in preparation for their discharge to the wider community. This is done through the "welfare group". This paper explores the therapeutic underpinnings of this ostensibly practical group and its fit within the philosophy of the therapeutic community.*


♦ Norton, K. (1996) **Management of difficult personality disorder patients**. *Advances in Psychiatric Treatment* Vol.2: pp 202-210
*Aimed at the general psychiatrist this paper describes the difficulties which arise from interpersonal aspects of working with personality disordered clients who have attachment problems relating to problematic childhoods which affect the treatment relationship. This paper also addresses strategies to combat these problems including diagnosis, engagement, medication, and treatment contracts.*

♦ Norton, K. & Hinshelwood, R. (1996) **Severe personality disorder: Treatment issues and selection for inpatient psychotherapy.** *British Journal of Psychiatry* Vol.168 (6): pp 725-733
*Written with the then Clinical Director of the Cassel Hospital, the position of the general psychiatry team to plan long term treatment for Severely personality disordered patients who are difficult to engage in consistent treatments in acute inpatient settings but whose mistrust of professionals is reinforced by inconsistencies in such situations is emphasised in this paper. A case is made for the advantages of specialist inpatient units and a plea for collaboration between specialist and non-specialist services is made.*

♦ Dolan, B.M., Morton, A., Wilson, J. (1990) **Selection of Admissions to a Therapeutic Community using a Group Setting: Association with degree and type of psychological distress.** *International Journal of Social Psychiatry.* Vol.36 (4): pp 265-271
*A comparison of those selected and rejected for admission by the 'selection group' (comprising current residents and staff) found no difference on global SCL-90R scores. However those not selected had higher sub-scale scores for somatisation, obsessive compulsion and phobic anxiety. These can be seen as symptoms which allow the sufferer to avoid verbalisation of their distress.*

♦ Warren, F. (1994) **What do we mean by a Therapeutic Community for offenders?** *Therapeutic Communities* Vo.15 (4): pp 312-319

♦ Parker, M. (1989) **Managing separation: The Henderson Hospital leavers group.** *International Journal of Therapeutic Communities* Vol.10 (1): pp 5-15
*Discusses the central role of the leavers group at Henderson in preparing resident, both practically and emotionally, for life outside the community.*

♦ Beach, K. (1988) **Therapeutic Factors in Group Psychotherapy.** *Community Psychiatric Nursing Journal* April, pp 5-15

♦ Whiteley, J.S., Collis, M. (1987) **Therapeutic factors applied to group psychotherapy in a therapeutic community.** *International Journal of Therapeutic Communities* Vo.8 (1): pp 21-31
*Bloch's method of assessing the 'most important event' in therapy found that learning from: interpersonal actions; acceptance; self-understanding were the most prominent*

*therapeutic factors in Henderson treatment. However, half of these 'most important events' happened outside the "formal therapy" groups but within the therapeutic community, emphasising the importance of the 24 hour sociotherapy.*

♦ Collis, M. (1987) **Women's groups in the therapeutic community: The Henderson experience** *International Journal of Therapeutic Communities,* Vol.8 (1): pp 175-184
*Describes the establishment of the Henderson women's group and analyses the ill-fated attempts by both men and women staff to determine the role of the group and the gradual evolution of a group culture based on the needs of the women themselves.*

♦ Beach, K. (1987) **Gender Roles in the Therapeutic Community.** *International Journal of Therapeutic Communities,* Vol.8 (1): pp 33-45
*This paper considers gender stereotypes within the therapeutic community and their defensive and oppressive functions. Attitudes and personal experiences of the male and female staff were measured alongside patterns of verbal communication.*

♦ Wilson, J. (1985) **Leaving Home as a Theme in a Therapeutic Community.** *International Journal of Therapeutic Communities* Vol.6 (2): pp 71-78
*Examines how problems and issues related to leaving home can be explored and resolved within a therapeutic community setting which acts as a transition between the family and the outside world.*

## PSYCHODRAMA AND ART THERAPY

♦ Hamer, N. (1993) **Some connections between Art Therapy and Psychodrama in a Therapeutic Community** *Inscape: Journal of the British Association of Art Therapists.* Winter: pp 23-26
*Updates the history and context of psychodrama at Henderson Hospital and explores the overlap with the current Art Work Group.*

♦ Mahoney, J (1992) **The organisational context of Art Therapy.** Chapter in *Handbook of Art Therapy,* D.Waller and A. Gilroy (eds.) Open University Press.
*An important paper which overviews the history of Henderson Hospital and discusses art therapy within the unit in the context of this history.*

♦ Hamer, N. (1990) **Group Analytic Psychodrama** *Group Analysis.* Vol.23 (3): pp 245-254
*Outlines the kind of psychodrama currently practised at Henderson Hospital and places this in the context of related work in psychodrama, group analysis and psychoanalysis.*

♦ Hamer, N. (1989) **Psychodrama in a Therapeutic Community** *Journal of the British Psychodrama Association.* Vol.4 (1): pp 23-40
*Details the historical development of psychodrama at Henderson Hospital.*

*See also these earlier key papers*

♦ Baker, A.A. (1952) **The misfit family: A psychodramatic technique used in a therapeutic community.** *British Journal of Medical Psychology* Vol.25 (3): pp 235-243
*A description of one of the early serial plays enacted by one shift of staff.*

♦ Jones, M. (1949) **Acting as an aid to therapy in a neurosis centre.** *British. Medical Journal* Vol. 1: pp 756-761
*Describes the varieties of psychodrama used in the early days of the unit, including patient produced plays, staff re-enactments of assessments and 'spontaneous' acting within small group analytic settings*

♦ Jones, M. (1948) **Emotional Catharsis and Re-education in the Neuroses with the Help of Group Methods.** *British Journal of Medical Psychology,* Vol. 21 (2): pp 104-110
*An early description of psychodrama in the context of other 'acting-out' in the unit.*

## THE OUTCOME OF TREATMENT

♦ Dolan, B. and Norton, K. (1998) **'Audit and Survival: Specialist In-patient Psychotherapy in the NHS'** In: *Reconstructing Audit: The case of psychotherapy services in the NHS* Eds. Patrick, M. and Davenhill, R. Routledge, London.

♦ Dolan, B, Warren, F, Norton, K. (1997) **Change in borderline symptoms one year after therapeutic community treatment for**

**severe personality disorder.** *British Journal of Psychiatry*, Vol. 171: pp 274-279

*This paper presents the principal outcome results of the most recent follow-up study of Henderson Hospital treatment (begun in 1990). The study improved on the methodology used in previous studies in various ways including using a variety of psychological and behavioural outcomes, collecting data both from patients and from their referrers and GPs, and using a comparison group. This, the outcome of borderline symptomatology shows very encouraging results for the therapeutic community versus treatment as usual.*

♦  Dolan, B.M., Evans, C., Wilson, J. (1992) **Therapeutic community treatment for personality disordered adults: Changes in neurotic symptomatology on follow-up.** *International Journal of Social Psychiatry*
Vol.38 (4): pp 243-250

*Demonstrates a highly significant reduction in symptomatic psychological distress between admission and eight month follow-up using the SCL-90R questionnaire. Considering individual change, 55% had improved statistically reliably and in 32% the improvement was also clinically significant. Only 6.5% had deteriorated since admission.*

♦  Dolan, B.M., Evans, C.D.H., Wilson, J. (1992) **Neurotic symptomatology and length of stay in a therapeutic community** *Therapeutic Communities* Vol.13 (3): pp 171-177

*Data from the SCL-90R questionnaire showed that length of stay in therapy was not related to initial symptomatology but could be predicted by changes in the first three months.*

♦  Norris, M. (1983) **Changes in patients during treatment at Henderson Hospital therapeutic community during 1977-1981.** *British Journal of Medical Psychology* Vol.56: pp 135-143

*A repertory grid study recorded significant changes in a sample of 103 residents during treatment in terms of their self-esteem; percept of self; percept of ideal self; aspirations regarding rule-breaking and independence. Over a three month treatment period 60% of residents improved on at least three of these five aspects.*

♦  Copas, J.B., O'Brien, M., Roberts, J.C., Whiteley, J.S. (1984) **Treatment outcome in personality disorder: The effect of social,**

**psychological and behavioural variables.** *Personality and Individual Differences* Vol.5: pp 565-573

*A follow-up study of 194 admitted and 51 non-admitted referrals showed significantly greater reduction in re-offending and hospital re-admission in the treated than in the untreated sample. The study showed that success rate increased with time spent in treatment, with 65% of those who stayed over 9 months being free of relapse five years after discharge.*

*See also these earlier key papers*

♦ Whiteley, J.S. (1970) **The response of psychopaths to a Therapeutic Community** *British Journal of Psychiatry* Vol.116: pp 517-529

*A follow-up study of 122 consecutive discharges showed that after 2 years 57.5% had no further psychiatric admissions 43.6% were free of re-conviction. Prognostic factors are also considered and a description of the unit, treatment programme and staff team in 1969 is appended.*

♦ Copas, J., Whiteley, J.S. (1976) **Predicting success in the treatment of psychopaths** *British Journal of Psychiatry* Vol.129: pp 388-392

*Expands on study by Whiteley (1970) above in examining factors in social history related to success or failure (re-conviction and re-admission). Based upon the subjects': marital history; employment record; academic achievement; previous psychiatric and criminal history, a prediction formula is given developed which is reliable at a significance level of 1%..*

# AUDIT OF THE E.C.R. PROCESS AND FUNDING ISSUES

♦ Dolan, B., Warren, F., Menzies, D., Norton, K. (1996) **Cost-offset following specialist treatment of severe personality disorders** *Psychiatric Bulletin* Vol.20: pp 7

*In a follow-up to Menzies et al.,(1993) the psychiatric and prison service usage of 24 patients was established for one year pre- and one year post-treatment at Henderson. The average annual cost was £13,966 pre-treatment compared to £1,308 post treatment representing a cost-offset of £12,658 per patient. The average cost of the specialist admission was £25,641. Thus the cost of treatment would be re-couped within two years and represent a saving thereafter.*

♦ Dolan B.M., Evans C., Norton K. (1994) **Funding treatment of offender patients with severe personality disorder: Do financial considerations trump clinical need ?** *Journal of Forensic Psychiatry* Vol. 5 2) pp 263-274

*A comparison of patients who were refused funding for their treatment with those admitted to Henderson Hospital showed no difference between the groups in personality disorder diagnosis, motivation, self-esteem, neurotic distress, previous psychiatric history or offending history. It is suggested that decisions to refuse funding are made on financial rather than clinical grounds. In addition those seen as 'offenders' may be less likely to obtain treatment as indicated those refused funding being more often on probation at referral.*

♦ Dolan B. (1993) **Mental Health and the Market: The case of Henderson Hospital** *The Health Summary* Vol. X (1): pp 6-7

♦ Menzies D., Dolan B., Norton K. (1993) **Funding treatment for personality disorders: Are short term savings worth long term costs?** *Psychiatric Bulletin* Vol.17: pp 517-519

*The first British paper to assess the financial cost of personality disordered patients to the Nation showed that in the one year preceding admission to Henderson a cohort of 29 residents had used a total of £423,115 worth of psychiatric and prison services*

♦ Norton. K., McGauley G., Wilson J., Menzies D. (1992) **Health care services in the market place: Early effects on caring relationships** *Therapeutic Communities* Vol.13 (4): pp 243-252

*Discusses the clinical implications of the NHS funding changes, in particular the impact of the 'patient as consumer' on caring relationships including the negative counter-transference reactions with personality disordered clients.*

♦ Dolan B.M., Norton K. (1992) **One year after the NHS Bill: The extra-contractual referral system at Henderson Hospital** *Psychiatric Bulletin* Vol.16: pp 745-747

*This and the two following papers, which can be read as a set, discuss the role of Henderson as a specialist personality disorder service within the NHS and the impact of the purchaser-provider changes on such units. The impact of the NHS funding changes are considered through an audit of the views of clinicians and an evaluation of the actual impact of the new contracting system on subsequent referral rates.*

♦ Dolan B.M., Norton K. (1991) **The predicted impact of the NHS bill on the use and funding of a specialist service for personality disordered patients: A survey of clinicians' views.** *Psychiatric Bulletin* Vol.15: pp 402-404

♦ Dolan B.M., Norton K. (1990) **Is there a need for specialist psychiatric units in the NHS? Henderson Hospital: A case in point.** *Psychiatric Bulletin* Vol.14: pp 72-76

# PERSONALITY DISORDER AND PSYCHOLOGICAL CHARACTERISTICS OF CLIENTS

♦ Warren, F., Dolan, B., & Norton, K. (1998) **Bloodletting, Bulimia Nervosa and Borderline Personality Disorder.** *European Eating Disorders Review,* Vol.6 (4): pp 277-285
*Controlled release of blood, using syringes or cannulae had been noted as a rare phenomenon associated with eating disorder. This paper suggests that this phenomenon may be more closely related to personality pathology and self-harming than eating disorder per se.*

♦ Norton, K. (1997) **In the prison of personality disorder.** *The Journal of Forensic Psychiatry*, Vol.8: No.2: September 1997
*Personality disordered patients can exhibit a "behavioural camouflage" which masks (or imprisons) their painful mental states. Aspects of the therapeutic community method of treatment which help to understand these processes and the implications for non-specialist settings including secure psychiatric facilities are discussed.*

♦ Norton K., Dolan B. (1996) **Personality Disorders and their Effect upon Parenting.** *Mentally Disordered Parents* Chapter 18 pp 219-232. Gopfert M, Webster J. & Seeman M (eds.). Cambridge, C.U.P.
*Outlines aspects of personality disorder that may lead to difficulties and deficits in the parenting-parented process. Clinical examples indicate how negative childhood experiences are reproduced when the personality disordered individual becomes a parent.*

♦ Norton K. (1996) **The Personality Disordered Forensic Patient and the Therapeutic Community.** Chapter in: Cox M. & Cordess C. (eds.) *Forensic Psychotherapy* London, Jessica Kingsley.
*Detailed exploration of some of the fundamental disturbance in personality disordered forensic patients and the ways in which the therapeutic community can be used to ameliorate these with examples*

♦ Dolan, B.M., Evans, C.D., Norton, K. (1995) **Multiple Axis-II diagnoses of personality disorder.** *British Journal of Psychiatry* Vol.106: pp 107-112
*A study shows high rates of multiple diagnoses of personality disorder in referrals to Henderson compared with a probation and general population sample. It is suggested that such multiple diagnosis is indicative of the breadth of pathology and may prove to be an important factor in treatment and prognosis.*

♦ Wesby R., Menzies D., Dolan B., Norton K. (1995) **A survey of psychological types in a therapeutic community.** *Therapeutic Communities,* Vol.16 (4): pp 229-238
*An investigation of 'Jungian' personality typology of Henderson staff and residents showed striking similarities between the two groups with the majority of community members showing introverted attitudes and a preference for intuitive modes of functioning.*

♦ Dolan B.M. & Merton Probation Centre Staff (1995) **The attribution of blame for criminal acts: relationship of personality disorder and mood.** *Criminal Behaviour and Mental Health,* Vol.5: pp 41-51

♦ Dolan B.M., Mitchell. E., (1994) **Personality disorders, psychological and behavioural characteristics of in women in the medical unit of HMP Holloway: A comparison with women in specialist NHS treatment** *Criminal Behaviour and Mental Health,* Vol.4 (2): pp 130-142

♦ Dolan B.M., Evans C., Norton K. (1994) **Eating disorders in male and female patients with personality disorders** *Journal of Personality Disorders,* Vol.6 (1): pp 17-25

*A survey of 130 adults referred to Henderson shows high rates of eating disorder symptoms in both men (9%) and women (37%). In the majority of these cases eating disorders have not previously been diagnosed.*

♦ Dolan B.M., Evans C., Norton K. (1992) **The separation individuation inventory: Association with borderline phenomena** *Journal of Nervous and Mental Diseases,* Vol.180 (8): pp 529-533
*Adult manifestations of separation-individuation difficulties are shown to be associated with two borderline personality measures. The psychometric properties of the instruments are also examined*

♦ Norton K.R.W. (1992) **'The Health of the Nation': The impact of personality disorder on 'key areas'.** *Postgraduate Medical Journal,* Vol.68: pp 350-354
*Documents how personality disorder is an invisible factor in much ill health (both mental and physical) and thus can have a far-reaching impact on different 'key areas' identified in the 'Health of the Nation' report, including: eating and drinking habits; smoking; prevention of accidents; suicide and HIV/AIDS.*

♦ Gudjønsson G.H., Roberts J.C. (1985) **Psychological and physiological characteristics of personality disordered patients.** Chapter in: Farrington D.P., Gunn J. (Eds.) *Aggression and Dang*erousness, Chichester, J. Wiley & Son Ltd.
*This chapter recounts a series of research studies using psychological tests and measuring electrodermal reactivity. The Hare-Cleckley description of the psychopath as lacking anxiety, affect or guilt is not supported by these studies of Henderson residents.*

♦ Gudjønsson G.H., Roberts J.C. (1982) **Guilt and self concept in psychopaths.** *Personality and Individual Differences,* Vol.4: pp 65 70
*This study suggests that guilt expressed by 'secondary psychopaths' at Henderson is related to a high level of trait anxiety and a low self-concept which may be a reflection of their disturbed family background and the constant disapproval which their behaviour creates.*

♦ Whiteley J.S. (1982) **Assessing dangerousness in psychopaths.** Chapter in: Hamilton J., Freeman H.(eds.) *Dangerousness: Psychiatric Assessment and Management*, London, Gaskell.

♦ Gudjønsson G.H., Roberts J.C. (1981) **The aggressive behaviour of personality disordered patients and its relation to personality and perceptual motor performance.** *Current Psychological Research,* Vol. 1 (2): pp 101-109

♦ Gudjønsson. G. H., Roberts. J. C. (1981) **Trail Making Scores as a Prediction of Aggressive Behaviour in Personality-Disordered Patients.** *Perceptual and Motor Skills*, Vol.52: pp 413-414

## RESEARCH ISSUES

♦ Norton, K., Dolan, B. (1995) **Assessing change in personality disorder.** *Current Opinion in Psychiatry,* Vol. 8 (6): pp 371-375
*Assessing change in core personality disorder phenomena is hampered by the scarcity of baseline severity data and the use of indirect measures of personality disorder which are not conceptually linked to the treatment focus. A more rational, systematic and collaborative approach to assessing change is suggested so that research in the field can progress.*

♦ Evans C., Carlyle J., Dolan B. (1996) **Forensic Psychotherapy Research** Chapter in: Cox M. & Cordess C. (eds.) *Forensic Psychotherapy,* London, Jessica Kingsley.
*Explores the difficulties inherent in evaluating psychoanalytically oriented treatment of offenders and outlines the various research methodologies which may be of future use in the emerging discipline of forensic psychotherapy.*

Dolan B. (1996) **Assessing Change: Lessons from the literature.** Chapter in: *Understanding the Enigma: Personality Disorder and Offending,* SHSA, London

*See also this earlier key paper*

♦ Manning N. (1979) **The politics of survival: the role of research in the therapeutic community.** Chapter 27 in: Hinshelwood R. and

Manning N. (eds.) *Therapeutic Communities: Reflections and Progress*, pp 287-296, Routledge, London.
*Discusses the role of research in the processes surrounding the survival of TCs using specific examples which illustrate the importance of early research work from Henderson Hospital.*

## STAFF ROLES AND TRAINING

♦ Reay, A., Revel, J. (1999) **Social therapists: Being real and being therapeutic** *Therapeutic Communities* (1999), Vol. 20 (2): pp 93-102

♦ Fainman D. (1995) **Quo Vadis in the Therapeutic Community: Leadership and training for what ?** *Therapeutic Communities*, Vol.16 (2): pp 103-111
*Argues that current leadership in TCs is pulled between clinical and managerial constraints as survival in the marketplace continually needs to be justified. The implications for trainees are discussed with particular reference to issues faced by senior registrars in psychotherapy.*

♦ Norton, K., Fainman, D. (1994) **Applications of the Therapeutic Community Concept: Dynamic Psychotherapy Training** *Therapeutic Communities*, Vol. 15 (2): pp 99-105

♦ Azu-Okeke, O. (1993) **Conflict in the search for an individual self as opposed to a traditional group self: A consequence of undertaking group analytic training** *Group Analysis*, Vol. 26: pp 261-268

♦ Azu-Okeke, O. (1992) **Experiments with Nigerian village communities in the dual roles of Western psychiatric treatment centres and homes for indigenous Nigerian inhabitants** *Therapeutic Communities* Vol.13 (4): pp 221-229
*Presents an account of two experiments of Therapeutic Community Models in an African Culture. The paper discusses how native inhabitants' functions complemented the professional staff functions in a village setting and how the village communities complemented a conventional psychiatric hospital.*

- Joughin N. (1990) **Henderson Hospital: A trainee's experience** *Psychiatric Bulletin,* Vol.14: pp 80-82
  *A trainee psychiatrists; personal commentary on six month placement at Henderson reflecting on how the attachment gave him new perspectives on 'responsibility'*

- Kynaston. T. , Meade. H., Jackman. K. (1981) **The Henderson Hospital: Nursing in a Therapeutic Community.** *Nursing,* Vol.30: pp 1328-1329
  *Describes the unique nursing process at Henderson Hospital and the role of the nurses within the multi-disciplinary team.*

*See also these earlier key papers*

- Whiteley J.S. (1978) **The dilemmas of leadership in the therapeutic community and the large group.** *Group Analysis,* Vol.11 (1): pp 40-47

- Sanders, R.M. (1973) **The role of a social therapist in a therapeutic community.** *Nursing Times,* December 20/27: pp 1746-1747

- Whiteley J.S., Zlatic M. (1972) **A re-appraisal of staff attitudes to the therapeutic Community** *British Journal of Social Psychiatry,* Vol.3 (2): pp 76-81

## BOOKS FROM HENDERSON HOSPITAL

Smith, S & Norton, K. (1999) **Counselling Skills For Doctors.** Open University Press

Norton, K. & McGauley, G. (1997) **Counselling Difficult Patients.** London: Sage.

Norton K. & Smith S. (1994) **Problems with Patients: Managing Complicated Transactions.** Cambridge University Press, Cambridge

Dolan B. (Ed.) (1994) **Therapeutic Communities for Offenders.** Therapeutic Communities: Special Edition 15, ATC, London

Dolan B. & Gitzinger I. (1994) **Why Women? Gender Issues and Eating Disorders.** Athlone Press, London.

Dolan B. & Coid J. (1993) **Psychopathic and Anti-social Personality Disorders: Treatment and Research Issues.** Gaskell, London

Whiteley J.S. (Ed.) (1991) **A Commemoration of Maxwell Jones.** International Journal of Therapeutic Communities: Special Edition 12, ATC, London

Whiteley J.S. & Gordon J (1979) **Group Approaches in Psychiatry.** Routledge and Kegan Paul, London.

Whiteley J.S., Briggs D. & Turner M. (1972 ) **Dealing with Deviants.** Hogarth Press, London.

Rapoport R. (1960) **Community as Doctor.** Tavistock, London.

Jones M. (1952) **Social Psychiatry: A study of Therapeutic Communities.** Tavistock, London.

*SEE ALSO*

Jones M. (1968) **Beyond the Therapeutic Community: Social Learning and Social Psychiatry.** Yale Univ. Press, New Haven & London.

Jones M. (1962) **Social Psychiatry in the Community, in Hospitals and in Prisons.** Charles C. Thomas, Illinois.